Clutter Intervention

About the Author

Tisha Morris is an author, speaker, and trainer in the healing arts. She is certified in feng shui, life coaching, energy healing, and yoga. Prior to her holistic work, Tisha practiced law and obtained a fine arts degree in interior design.

As a feng shui expert, interior designer, and energy healer, Tisha combines traditional feng shui techniques, design aesthetics, and intuition to turn challenging spaces into supportive environments to help improve the lives of all those who live and encounter the space.

Tisha works with homeowners, businesses, real estate agents, corporations, land builders, and non-profit organizations to help improve spaces by using feng shui, space clearing, interior design, interior decorating, clutter clearing, five-element analysis, and land healing.

Tisha is based in Los Angeles and works one-on-one with clients in their homes and businesses and also facilitates workshops and certification trainings. She is the founder of Earth Home School of Feng Shui and Feng Shui for the Planet, a foundation to help promote better living spaces across the globe. For more information, visit www.earthhome.tv.

Clutter Intervention

HOW YOUR STUFF IS KEEPING YOU STUCK

TISHA MORRIS

Llewellyn Publications
Woodbury, Minnesota

First Edition
First Printing, 2018

Cover design by Shira Atakpu

Llewellyn Publications is a registered trademark of Llewellyn Worldwide Ltd.

Library of Congress Cataloging-in-Publication Data
Names: Morris, Tisha, author.
Title: Clutter intervention : how your stuff is keeping you stuck / Tisha Morris.
Description: First edition. | Woodbury, Minnesota : Llewellyn Publications, [2018]
Identifiers: LCCN 2017044487 (print) | LCCN 2017047378 (ebook) | ISBN 9780738754468 (ebook) | ISBN 9780738753263 (alk. paper)
Subjects: LCSH: Storage in the home. | Orderliness. | House cleaning. | Personal belongings--Psychological aspects.
Classification: LCC TX309 (ebook) | LCC TX309 .M67 2018 (print) | DDC 648/.8—dc23
LC record available at https://lccn.loc.gov/2017044487

Llewellyn Worldwide Ltd. does not participate in, endorse, or have any authority or responsibility concerning private business transactions between our authors and the public.

All mail addressed to the author is forwarded but the publisher cannot, unless specifically instructed by the author, give out an address or phone number.

Any Internet references contained in this work are current at publication time, but the publisher cannot guarantee that a specific location will continue to be maintained. Please refer to the publisher's website for links to authors' websites and other sources.

Llewellyn Publications
A Division of Llewellyn Worldwide Ltd.
2143 Wooddale Drive
Woodbury, MN 55125-2989
www.llewellyn.com

Printed in the United States of America

Other Books by Tisha Morris

Decorating With the Five Elements of Feng Shui

Mind, Body, Home: Transform Your Life One Room at a Time

Feng Shui Your Life: The Quick Guide to Decluttering Your Home and Renewing Your Life

27 Things to Feng Shui Your Home

This book is dedicated to my mom and dad.
I am forever grateful for your role in helping me
create a foundation of what home is.
Wherever I go, you are with me and I am always home.

Acknowledgments

The decluttering process is not just about letting go—it's a discovery of what's truly important to you. The years leading up to writing this book were filled with both. In 2012, I sold everything and drove cross-country to Los Angeles to start over. Since then, I've moved six times—each with new considerations of what to keep and what to let go of.

The impetus to writing this book, however, was the sudden passing of my mom. When I looked at the things she left behind, I began to see our stuff through a different lens. I began to see how we fill our homes and our lives with fillers. We are living amongst our own cover-up.

What are we covering up? It's unique to each of us, and the journey is yours to discover. You will find your authentic self at the bottom of the pile. And what is most enriching to you will rise to the surface and be mirrored in all areas, especially the people in your life. It is those people I would like to acknowledge.

Thank you to everyone at Llewellyn Publications, especially Angela Wix. I appreciate the continued support beyond words.

I want to give a long overdue acknowledgment to Theda Day. You have been an unwavering fan, friend, confidante, catalyst, and general coconspirator to this crazy life. Most of all, you have been my witness. Thank you.

I also want to thank my soulstice sister, Kellen Brugman, for sharing this journey with me. You blazed the trail and then walked with me during the best and worst of days.

I also want to thank my sister and family—Leslie, Bobby, Joshua, and Erica—for being a rock when I felt like sand.

And finally, I want to thank Rachel Lang for picking me up on that fateful day at the airport when I truly needed picking up. You continue to show up when I need you the most. Your support, encouragement, and love are unending, and I am so grateful to have you as a partner. I love you and all your kitchen gadgets with all my heart. One day I will write a love story and it will be for you.

Until then, I write about spaces and how we can use them to heal our life. I want to thank you—the reader—for investing your time and energy in reading this book. I think you will find it life-changing. I hope so. I want you to live out your wildest dreams. Go forth and let go. Create space for your true love—yourself.

Contents

Contents

Contents

Introduction

In 2010, I released my first book, *Feng Shui Your Life: The Quick Guide to Decluttering Your Home and Renewing Your Life*, which dealt primarily with the practicalities of decluttering. After releasing past relationships through my own decluttering process, I understood and appreciated the power of releasing the past and wanted to share the benefits I experienced.

In my subsequent books, *Mind, Body, Home: Transform Your Life One Room at a Time* and *Decorating With the Five Elements of Feng Shui*, I explored all facets of feng shui and the nuances of energy in our spaces. I enjoyed the break from writing and teaching about clearing clutter and honestly had no intention of revisiting the topic. That is, until January 2016, when my mom suddenly passed away.

I grew up in a neat and orderly home. I learned organization and proper decorating by example from my mom. Home was always a place of pride, from decorating tours to entertaining friends. In fact, I often wondered why the topic of decluttering had become such a big part of my work. Anytime I facilitated a feng shui workshop, regardless of the intended topic, it inevitably came around to questions about clearing clutter. I've always been conscientious about my stuff, making routine donation drop-offs. Usually, you teach what you most need to learn. What did I need to learn?

My mom passed away at age seventy-six, just three weeks after being diagnosed with an aggressive form of leukemia. Aside from the shock and grief, my sister and I were left with taking over my mom's day-to-day tasks, which included taking care of my dad with his own set of health challenges. Like most children whose parents have passed, we found dealing with the logistical aftermath overwhelming.

As my sister and I began tackling the household responsibilities that my mom had neatly left in her typical organized fashion, I was taken aback when I started really looking at the house with new eyes. I had seen it through my child eyes, my adult eyes, and even my feng shui eyes. My mom had designed the house and had been practicing feng shui without realizing it. After reading my books, she delighted in the fact that she had been using feng shui all along. But what lay behind closed doors was another story.

As I opened the closets, as I had hundreds of times, I was now seeing them as the closets of someone whose life had been covered up with layers of stuff. What was it covering up? If my mom had been my client, I would have recommended a major decluttering immediately. Every closet was packed to the brim. The organization disguised the clutter.

Beneath the rubble of stuff is the reality
at the heart of our pain. It hides the truth,
keeps our shadows dark, and preserves
our state of denial.

It didn't end there. Without my mom to keep things organized, my dad's true colors quickly began to show. Papers—stacks and stacks of papers—everywhere. I flashed back to the days of seeing his office, a domain my mom didn't have control over. It was a paper explosion. The illusion of order that I had grown up in was quickly replaced by the reality of two cofunctioning pack rats.

Of course, I wasn't off the hook either. For someone who prided themself on being clutter-free after selling everything and moving cross-country, I was shocked by what I found in the closet of my childhood room. Old skeletons and old identities still lingered. Any illusion of a normal, well-adjusted family unraveled before my eyes like a thread pulled from a tightly knit garment. The truth busted the seemingly invisible seams.

Clutter is the best evidence to identify what our blind spots are, where we are staying stuck in the past out of comfort and fear, and what identities we are still attached to that are no longer a part of our present life or desired future life.

What became evident was that clutter doesn't cause stagnation, delusion, fatigue, or illness—it's what shrouds the evidence of what lies at the bottom of the pile. It hides our blind spots. This starts the cycle of our stuff piling up and thereby keeping us stuck. Beneath the rubble of stuff is the reality at the heart of our pain. It hides the truth, keeps our shadows dark, and preserves our state of denial. As long as we are in denial, truth is not accessible and expansion cannot happen.

Everything in our home is a physical extension of ourselves and gives us clues to what we're holding on to in our unseen emotional and mental world. Clutter is the best evidence to identify what our blind spots are, where we are staying stuck in the past out of comfort and fear, and what identities we are still attached to that are no longer a part of our present life or desired future life.

When the underlying reason for holding on to something is revealed, the actual letting go is easy. And, as you let the item go, the underlying emotions related to it are instantly and simultaneously released. This is the magic of decluttering and the purpose of *Clutter Intervention*. Awareness brings transformation. Transformation allows you to step into the life that you truly want to be living and that is most authentic to you. And this is what I hope this book will bring you.

The average American home has tripled in size over the last fifty years and contains approximately 300,000 items.[1] And if that weren't enough stuff, off-site storage facilities have become the fastest-growing commercial real estate property.[2] I probably don't need to tell you that our stuff is becoming a big problem. It's most likely why you picked up this book. But what you probably don't know is the reason why you hold on to the things you hold on to. Once you know the *why*, the *how* to let go is easy.

Clearing clutter is similar to losing weight. There are a lot of how-to books on the best methods, but to do it effectively you must get to the root of the underlying issue of why you are holding on to the weight or, in this case, the clutter. Everyone knows how to lose weight: you eat less and exercise more. Everyone knows how to clear clutter: you put things you don't love or use in a bag and take it to a donation center. But why aren't we able to do these simple steps?

As a feng shui consultant, I've spent years helping people let go of stuff and have heard every excuse you could imagine for holding on to certain items. What I've noticed is that most people have

---

1. Mary MacVean, "For Many People, Gathering Possessions Is Just the Stuff of Life," *Los Angeles Times*, March 21, 2014.

2. John Mooallem, "The Self-Storage Self," *The New York Times Magazine*, September 2, 2009.

a strong desire to declutter because it's a natural process that feels good—that is, until emotional items rear their head. It just takes one or two items with emotional weight to stop us in our tracks and keep us from opening the next drawer or closet door. Our decluttering efforts come to a sudden halt, and we are left believing that we just don't have the desire or time. As a result, we continue to hold on to certain items that keep us stuck.

When the natural process of letting go is interrupted, we keep ourselves paralyzed in letting anything go. Before long, we feel stuck at home and in our life. And by "stuck" I mean not living the life we want to be living. Our home and our possessions are mirrors of ourselves. When we feel stuck amongst our stuff, we feel stuck in our life, particularly in those areas that the items represent. When we let go of items that keep us stuck, new energy suddenly enters that area of our life. In the following chapters, you will see how certain items relate to specific areas of your life.

But, first, why do we hold on to our stuff?

Our stuff is an external representation of who we are in the world. It represents our identity. Whether it's a photo album, an old pair of jeans, or an antique jewelry box, it's personal to who we are. The problem comes when our identity changes, as inevitably it does, through key life phases and experiences. But oftentimes our stuff doesn't change with it. When change happens, we hold on to our old identity through our stuff, grasping at the only sense of self that is familiar. This is when we get stuck. Stuck in the old identity. Stuck in our old life.

This book reveals the underlying identities to which we commonly cling, as well as their emotional counterparts, and how they show up as clutter in our spaces. Once you have awareness of the real issue, letting go is easy and decluttering can happen immediately, freeing you to live authentically. In understanding the underlying emotions at the bottom of the pile, you will then be able to tackle those areas of your home you've put off for years. In doing so, you will also breathe new energy into your life.

In chapter 1 you will see how your home is a mirror of your life. Everything in your home is an aspect of yourself—past, present, and future. Decluttering is as much about discerning what to let go of from your past as it is about what to keep. As you make these decisions, you are becoming more conscious of what you are ready to let go of in your life and what you are ready to embrace. Decluttering is not just a to-do list, but an intervention of what you truly desire in your life going forward.

Chapter 2 explains how significant changes in our life trigger identity crises. Although difficult, these changes are normal and for the purpose of our growth and expansion. With more perspective about these transitional times, it's possible to navigate them with more understanding and less stress. Letting go of the past is essential to fully stepping into the next phase of life. Decluttering items relating to the old identity is essential for a graceful transition.

Chapters 3 through 6 cover common identities, from past relationships to past careers to past grievances, that we hold on to and the correlating stuff representing those identities that keep us stuck in the past. Chapter 7 looks at current identities that are out of balance. Wonder why you continue finding yourself with too much of a particular type of item, such as magazines, beauty products, or clothing accessories? These items represent a current identity, but the excess represents an overcompensation that will be discussed in more detail.

In chapter 8, your clutter intervention continues by debunking the most common excuses used when it comes to decluttering. What's really going on when you hear yourself say, "I might need this broken blender *just in case*" or "I don't want to add more stuff to the landfill"? It can be challenging to get perspective when it comes to our own stuff. We can really trick ourselves into justifying certain items. But after reading this chapter, you will be able to once and for all understand what's at the heart of the matter. Clutter excuses begone.

Chapter 9 explores our next big problem—digital clutter—and what to do about it. Just because clutter is out of sight, it doesn't mean it's out of mind. Instead, we've just expanded our clutter storage. We have clutter not only in our filing cabinets, but in our computer files too. And that's just the beginning with the infinitely expanding virtual cloud.

By chapter 10, you will have a clear understanding of why you've been holding on to certain items, along with the common excuses and saboteurs that have until now kept you stuck. Now it's time to roll up your sleeves and get busy on the physical level. Chapter 10 provides a practical, step-by-step approach to clearing clutter, in addition to an intuitive approach of listening to your body.

When it comes to clutter, the more you understand the psychological and emotional components underlying your stuff, the easier it will be when it comes time to putting things in a bag. In doing so, you will begin to feel lighter and freer with each item. Like a snake shedding its skin, you can move into a new phase of life with ease and grace, with your home reflecting who you really are and want to be.

CHAPTER 1

Your Home Is a Mirror
What Are You Projecting?

In my previous book, *Mind, Body, Home,* each part of the house is broken down into the correlating mental, emotional, and physical counterpart of ourselves. Even the fascia of a house takes on a form similar to the human face with the front door as the mouth, the windows as the eyes, and the roof as the head. It's no coincidence that the home has been used as a metaphor for our mind or body in religions, mythologies, and dream symbols for thousands of years.

Our home is an energetic extension of ourselves with every aspect reflected somewhere in it. This is made even more exact by the stuff we possess. Every item is an expression or extension of our mental and emotional selves. This is why decluttering can be such an arduous process. You are literally letting go of mental and emotional aspects of yourself. The only variable is how active your emotional connection to a particular item is. Has it passed its expiration date in your life? Is it supporting you or keeping you stuck?

These questions may seem like a weighted conversation for a broken toaster tucked away in your kitchen cabinet or an old art project stored in the guest room closet. But not so when you consider that every item is taking up physical space in your home and energetic space in your mind. Even if it seems out of sight, your clutter is projecting this energy out into your life just like an outdated outfit or a broken car would.

Decluttering is serious energy work, not unlike going to an energy healer, acupuncturist, yoga class, therapist, or any other healing modality. This is why decluttering is so powerful and life changing. In all my work in the holistic arts, I have found decluttering to be the quickest way to make profound changes. You are literally removing old, stagnant energy to make space for new, fresh energy. For example, if you've been sending out résumés and going to job interviews, decluttering your office space will expedite the process. After creating space, new energy in the form of phone calls and job offers can now come in.

Clutter is the physical representation of our emotional and mental blocks, and once it is removed, change can happen fast. We ultimately manifest our life from our mental and emotional bodies. The removal of clutter literally frees those areas of our psyche like removing the wall of a dam to allow water to flow through once again. As you become more aware of what items are blocking your energy, you can begin to use your home as a manifesting tool to attract more of what you want in your life.

Using Your Home to Manifest Your Life

The law of attraction has become the predominant concept for manifestation among spiritual and self-help communities. Manifestation is the process of turning ideas and thoughts into physical form. As spiritual beings having a physical experience, we are all alchemists turning nonphysical concepts into physical objects for survival and enjoyment on earth. It is through the law of attraction that we create our own reality—from the home we live in, to the car we drive, to the relationships we attract into our life.

At the root of the law of attraction is energy, or vibration. Like energy attracts like energy. If you are a vibrational match to a Mercedes, then you will attract a Mercedes to you. This also works on the emotional level. For example, if you are a vibrational match to abandonment as a result of childhood wounding, then you will attract more abandonment into your life through relationships. This will continue until the contrast becomes so stark that you consciously desire for something different. Once that desire becomes conscious, you will then attract the right people and situations to heal the past wounds.

You have manifested everything in your home with your thoughts and emotions. You wanted a comfy tan couch and made it happen by shopping, ordering, purchasing, and having it delivered. Everything in your home was a vibrational match to you at some point, and you attracted it to you. Yes, even your spouse or roommate. Your home is a giant composite of you. It's also a giant emitter of your energy. Think of it as a living vision board.

A vision board is a commonly used tool for activating or expediting the law of attraction. You can create a vision board by placing images or key words of what you want in your life onto a two-dimensional poster or mat board. In addition to consciously determining what you want, the subconscious mind responds well to the imagery on the board, similar to subliminal messages. Your home has the same effect. If you want to know what you're manifesting, look no further than your home.

Imagine pasting your home and all its contents on a flat board. Spread it out like a map of the world. Artwork, pictures, books, closets, cabinets, bedroom, office—they're all tangible representations of the energy you're beaming out into the world. Our world is a hologram that reflects back to us what we emit out. That which you put out comes back to you, and this is true for your home as well.

Look at your home objectively, not just the pretty parts, but the closets, cupboards, and clutter too. How is your home *not* in alignment with what you want? What needs to go? What is stuffed, cramped, outdated? What would be a better representation of you? Inspirational artwork, curtains you love instead of tolerate, current books, functional rooms? Are you in a transitional space that is currently serving you during a transitional time, or do you desire more permanence? Is it time to change some things on your virtual vision board?

If you've worked with a vision board or other law of attraction methods, you may have wondered why you manifest some things but not others. Either the desire wasn't truly there or, in most cases, there's an underlying subconscious block that is stronger. Our subconscious thoughts and beliefs that lie beneath the surface are as important as our conscious thoughts—actually, more so. Our subconscious thoughts make up approximately 95 to 99 percent of our thoughts and behaviors, and yet we have little awareness of them. They consist of past programming, influences from the collective conscious, and our shadow sides. These are sometimes referred to as our *blind spots* or *shadows* because they are below our conscious awareness.

The more we can become aware of and integrate our shadows, the more whole we will feel and the more precise our manifestations will become. The question is, how do we see what we can't see? This is the power of working with our home, which is a three-dimensional projection of ourselves. All your shadows are in your home. Are you wondering what yours are? The better question is, where in your home have you hidden them?

Shadow Work Through Space

Each room of the home represents a correlating aspect of ourselves, with the closet symbolizing what we would rather keep hidden. It's where we hide our shadows. It's no wonder we use the phrase "skeletons in the closet" to refer to things we keep hidden. And, of course, there is the common phrase "coming out of the closet," which refers to expressing an aspect of ourselves that we have kept hidden from the world.

We all have shadows or shadow sides. These are aspects of our personality that we have disassociated from or denied because at some point in childhood it was not safe for them to be seen. These aspects have been termed *shadows* or *shadow sides* because of our inability to see them. You can also think of it as a blind spot, your dark side, or the unconscious. The collective consciousness has a shadow side as well, commonly termed dark forces, dark energy, or even the devil.

In Taoist philosophy, the duality of light and dark, or yin and yang, is prevalent in everything. It only becomes a problem when we deem it bad or wrong and hide these aspects of ourselves, which then become shame. The more we hide them, the darker they become. This causes a division within the self. This is what leads to feeling inauthentic and generally dissatisfied with life. Instead of whole, we are fragmented.

Psychologist Carl Jung was the first to bring to light the impact of our shadow sides in the field of psychology. Many spiritual and self-help teachers have since integrated shadow work into spirituality, including Deepak Chopra, Debbie Ford, and Teal Swan. Becoming your whole self, in alignment with your soul, is at the crux of spirituality. To do so, your shadows must be integrated. Our shadows are also where our best gifts lie dormant. Carl Jung has been credited in calling our shadows the "seat of our creativity." It's usually those shadow aspects that make us unique, and it is our uniqueness that the world wants to see.

How do we work with something we can't see? Jung is also quoted as saying, "Until you make the unconscious conscious, it will direct your life and you will call it fate." Our shadows show up in our everyday life, including our projections onto other people. Those traits you most dislike in others are a good sign of your own shadows. For example, if someone with a boisterous personality annoys you, then you've most likely hidden a more outgoing aspect of yourself. You may have received punishment at a young age for acting out and this side of you was deemed bad. Being more outgoing and energetic is now a trait that not only would benefit you in some way, but would also bring more joy into your everyday life.

Unconscious shadows also show up in the home. We can bring our shadows into the light by working with our home, specifically with stuff we've stored in our closet or other storage areas. The closet is where we store items so that others can't see them, nor do we have to look at them ourselves. For those with limited closet space, it could be other storage spaces, such as the basement, storage shed, or even an off-site storage unit. I recently discovered shadow aspects of myself in the closet of my childhood room.

Out of the Closet and Into the Light

Before I share my experience, keep in mind that there's nothing wrong with storing items. Storage serves a really good purpose. We don't want to see our clothes strewn around the room or extra towels and toilet paper sitting out. Closets are great for keeping rooms clear of clutter, and off-site storage facilities are sometimes necessary during transitional times. But when storage becomes a permanent mausoleum for stuff from our past, then it's a red flag that we are storing things we don't want to deal with.

The phrase "coming out of the closet" is usually used in terms of announcing one's sexuality in terms of it being different from what's "normal." But there's more to "coming out" than an announcement to the world. It's an acknowledgment of oneself. At its core, it's self-acceptance. Imagine how amazing it would be if we all came out of the closet and accepted ourselves for who we really are.

I'm super short and love myself.

I am a big mouth and think I'm awesome.

I sing show tunes in the shower and think I sound pretty good.

I dress up in women's clothes and look stunning.

I didn't go to college and know I'm smart.

I can juggle while playing the harmonica and think I'm totally cool.

We hide aspects of ourselves not just from the world, but also from ourselves. What if these were in fact the more interesting parts of you? Most likely they are. However, we tend to believe our idiosyncrasies make it harder or impossible for us to fit in. As a result, we overcompensate for them and perhaps even have shame about them.

When I went back to Nashville due to my mother's passing, I spent a lot more time than usual at my family's home. It seemed like the perfect time to go through the few remaining belongings I had stored at their house. I was surprised when I stepped into the closet and sitting neatly on the shelf was a box labeled "Tisha crystal." How had I overlooked this box?

It was the never-used crystal from my wedding in 1998, a marriage that ended shortly thereafter in 2001. I'd moved more than a dozen times since then and released so many items from that relationship and many others. Somehow through all my purges, online sales, and moves, that box hadn't budged in fifteen years. The better question was, why were these items still in my childhood closet— never to have left?

I opened the lid of this Pandora's box. It was full of crystal wine glasses, still in original wrapping, with a few notecards still tucked in. They were relics from a time I thought I had fully dealt with, but the "Tisha crystal" box told a different story:

Guilt. The gifts. The failed marriage. The witnesses. The celebration. The disappointment. Disappointing my family. Failure.

Shame. The hiding. The shame. The hiding. The shame. Self-acceptance. Coming out. The rejection. Disgrace. Shame. Tolerance. Rejection. The trying. The nonconformist. Self-acceptance. Self-love. More self-love. Unconditional love.

Sitting on that shelf was the last shred of evidence of an old identity. It was liberating to finally get rid of that box—one that I could never fit into. It's a perfect example of believing that we've worked through issues only to find remnants or new layers we've not completely worked through. I share this story as an example of how our stuff can represent that last remaining percent of emotional energy that is awaiting completion and integration. Instead of the whole package, sometimes our stuff represents the red bow that needs to be tied up and finally handed off.

In order to transform anything, we have to bring it into the light —into our conscious awareness. We have to see it, acknowledge it, and accept it. This is exactly why our ego shoves our shadows in the dark of our closets or other unseen storage areas. The farther back, the better. And then we can remain in denial about emotions we don't want to deal with. When these shadow aspects are kept hidden over time, they fester and become regret, resentment, remorse, and rejection. These toxic emotions are the stepchildren of guilt and shame and are discussed in more detail in chapter 6.

The Fear of Empty Space

In addition to storing emotions in our closets, we also tend to fill just about any space we can find with our stuff. The predominant emotion in today's culture is feeling overwhelmed, and our homes generally mirror this trend. Most people complain about not having enough time in their day or space in their home. Our life is cluttered with time clocks, technology, and trying to maintain it all with our home reflecting this back to us. We are undergoing a cultural clutter epidemic on all levels. But it's not really about our stuff. It's about what our stuff is covering up.

While we complain about not having enough time or space, we stay busy trying to fill up both. Most of us feel a need to fill any bit of empty space we find—silence in conversation, an empty wall, a painting with just a brush stroke, an empty calendar. Empty space is uncomfortable for most people.

> But it's not really about
> our stuff. It's about what our stuff
> is covering up.

In art, empty space is called the *negative space*. In music, it's the pause just prior to a crescendo. In homes, it's the area where the space breathes. In meditation, it's the pause between the inhale and exhale. In Japanese art (one of the few cultures that value empty space), the void is called *ma* and is highly revered. In all art forms, the beauty lies in the empty space. Why then are we so uncomfortable with it while also craving it?

Fear breeds in empty space. It's where we can hear our thoughts. It forces us to look at our life. We have to witness the choices we've made. We have to remember the ungrieved past. To avoid this, we fill our homes and lives with stuff. We fill our calendar. We put a console along an empty wall. We fill quietness with idle chatter or TV noise. Before long, our lives become cluttered all in an unconscious attempt to avoid the emptiness.

Other words for empty space are *the gap, the void, the liminal,* or *nothingness.* This scares the hell out of us. In this state, the ego clamors for reassurance that it exists. There is a rush to fill the space with anything, even if it's not soul fulfilling. Anything not to have a black hole reflected at us. It's like walking down a dark hallway with no end. And so we fill our calendar and home with people, places, and things. Before long, our life is cluttered and we feel overwhelmed with stuff with little or no meaning. The ego is validated, but at a high price: *I'm overwhelmed and therefore I exist.*

The void is also where creation is born. The same place we find our fears is the place we find our soul. Follow the fear and you will find your authentic self. This is what we're truly afraid of. Finding our true self comes with moving out of our comfort zone, changing family beliefs, taking risks, being seen, and feeling vulnerable. The more these words scare you, the deeper your piles of clutter. Clutter is shallow; space is deep. Filling empty space is like filling the lungs with black balloons.

What I don't see, I don't have to deal with. The more I distract myself, the less likely I will have to see the truth.

Another common problem is when people allow others to fill their spaces. In an attempt to avoid emptiness or when we are unable to embody our own energy in the form of our own sense of power, we allow others to take our energy. This can show up in the form of other people's stuff stored in the home, burglars, or even rodents. If you are allowing unwanted energy in your home, then you are allowing unwanted energy in your life. This is a telltale sign of boundary issues that can show up in personal relationships or even with strangers. Are you allowing others to take up your space, your energy, your boundaries, and your preferences?

Most people struggle with either having too much space or not enough space. The amount of space that feels best is personal with no one-size-fits-all rule. The best barometer is to ask yourself questions: Do I feel stuck, scared, or free? Is my vision clear or clouded? Am I filling space out of fear or joy? From ego or soul? Out of anxiety or creativity? What am I really covering up? Whatever it is, there also lies a portal of beauty underneath. We all have a different standard of how much stuff we desire—in our home and on our calendar.

How Much Stuff Is Too Much?

It's common to think that dealing with clutter is dealing with an over-abundance of stuff. However, that's not always the case. The real problem could be a few items that are hidden away in a closet like a time capsule. In this case, the problem is harder to spot because it's been buried so deep in the psyche and therefore hidden or disguised in the home. The further away something is stored, the more we don't want to deal with it. This is often the location of the diamond in the rough that holds the key to unlocking the past in order to move forward.

Those who admit to having too much stuff with a desire to declutter are usually more conscious of their personal challenges. This allows for more self-growth and transformation, whereas the issues of those with organized clutter and the appearance of being clutter-free and in control of their life are more disguised and harder to consciously change. These people tend to store away their issues in drawers and closets in a neat and tidy manner.

For people who simply have too much stuff with no desire to address their discomfort, it's usually a subconscious tactic for covering up or distracting from the past to the point of affecting one's present level of happiness.[3] When one's living space is visually cluttered, the mind is cluttered. This strategically keeps people from having to look at their life. It's like turning the TV volume up loud so that you don't have to hear yourself think.

---

3. In characterizing people with too much stuff, I am not referring to those who may be clinically diagnosed with hoarding disorder. Hoarding disorder is a mental illness recognized by the American Psychiatric Association and is beyond the scope of this book, although some of the principles in this book may apply to those with hoarding disorder.

We all have a different standard for what is too much. Some people are minimalists and prefer sparser and clean-lined spaces, whereas others prefer more knick-knacks. What may seem cluttered to me may feel like a cozy haven to you. What may seem cold and stark to one person may feel liberating to another.

There are also cultural differences that can influence the amount of stuff we like to have in our living spaces. For example, spaces in England tend to be cozy and homey and could be considered cluttered to a minimalist. This is of course a generalization. It's no coincidence that the Victorian style of decorating, known for its bric-a-brac, began in England. Japanese culture, on the other hand, is known for its calm and minimalist spaces. For some, these spaces could feel barren and impersonal. Even within the United States styles vary, with climate being a major factor.

It's important to recognize your particular style, which is a by-product of your culture, familial environment, and personality type. When you know what feels good, you then know what doesn't feel good. And vice versa. The key is to know when too much is too much *for you*. When I work with clients with too much stuff, they are usually aware of it because they don't feel good in their home. They often comment that it feels like the walls are collapsing in on them. This is always a sign of what's showing up on the mental and emotional levels in the form of stagnation, confusion, emotional claustrophobia, regret, lack of direction, weight gain, or depression.

Your home should feel safe and
comfortable and also expansive
and liberating.

Finding this balance isn't always easy and requires an ongoing consciousness of your space and how you feel about it. Your home should feel safe and comfortable and also expansive and liberating. This is the beauty of using feng shui principles, not as a one-time application but as an ongoing practice. If you're not conscious of your space, then what are you conscious of? Aside from your mind and body, it is the only space you have any control over and is always a direct reflection of yourself.

As you read the succeeding chapters, be honest with yourself. Look at your home through an objective lens. Everything in your home is from the past. Unless you purchased or were given something today, then everything you own was acquired prior to this moment. Our lives are a collection of experiences up to this moment, and our belongings represent this. Our stuff contains stories, memories, and associations, some good and some not so good. At any moment, we have a choice to make a different decision, tell a different story, or take a new path.

By now you're starting to see that your belongings are not just household items sitting around but a mosaic of you. What from your past do you want to take forward? Which items are still relevant to you now and to where you want to go? By making no decision and keeping what you currently own, you are in effect making a decision to continue on as things have been. This is fine if that's what you want. But if you are tired of the old stories, the old patterns, the old thoughts, then it's time to dump the past.

When the past is so present that your
vision for your future is cloudy, fuzzy,
or overwhelming, that's when you know
too much is too much.

When the past is more present than it should be in your life, that's when you know too much is too much. This is when memorabilia becomes a rogue force keeping you stuck instead of a supportive platform from which to move forward. When the past is so present that your vision for your future is cloudy, fuzzy, or overwhelming, that's when you know too much is too much. That's when you know you've clung to the past out of fear of the unknown future. That's when it's time for a clutter intervention.

CHAPTER 2

Identity Crises

Who Am I?

If you've wondered how you have accumulated so much stuff through-out your life, you're not alone. This is a question most people ask them-selves at some point and is oftentimes the impetus for decluttering. We begin to feel overwhelmed by our possessions or even claustrophobic in our own space. Accumulation is a normal process, but so is letting go. When this becomes out of balance, the feeling is palpable. And be-cause our home is a mirror for our life, the inability to let go of things from the past becomes a bigger theme in our life.

You can look back at your own life and notice times when you owned few possessions and other times when you owned many. Most of us experience a natural ebb and flow of possessions as we move through different phases of life. That being said, accumulating items is easier and more familiar for many people than letting them go. The reason for this is discussed in more detail throughout this book. But first, we must understand why we want our stuff before we're willing to part with it.

We all experience significant identity shifts throughout our life. When our belongings don't change with us is when our stuff starts to pile up. This is where the cog gets stuck in the wheel in our own personal growth. Before we know it, we are stopped in our tracks with a decluttering project as we hold on tight to the stuff that represents our past identities. The questions "Who am I?" and "Why am I still holding on to this item?" are really one and the same.

Forming Identity Through Our Stuff

We come into this life to experience having a physical body in a three-dimensional world for the purpose of individuation. We are spiritual beings having a human experience. The tangible, three-dimensional world that we live in is an expression of our individuation—from what we wear to what we drive. It's normal to want, desire, and possess objects. It's part of the human experience and essential to our physical existence. Your desire for stuff didn't start last year or even last decade, but instead much earlier when the ego first formed.

Our desire for individuation begins around age two. This is a milestone developmental stage when identity, or ego, starts to form. We form the cognitive understanding that we are separate from other people and things. The first desire for independence rears its head. The terrible twos stage begins and perhaps never ends. Tangible objects that we perceived as a part of us now become separate from us. This is when ownership begins.

This is mine. Mine. Mine. Mine.

We begin to form our identity through our possessions. Our stuff helps differentiate me from you. My stuff expresses who I am. Our stuff also provides a mirror for our existence, especially when caregivers aren't immediately present. A teddy bear or blanket provides us comfort when needed. We feel safe with our things around us.

Our belongings are the few things that distinguish us from one another. After all, we share 99.9 percent of the same DNA as each other and 99 percent the same as chimpanzees. Giving up a red ball at two years old or your lettermen jacket at age forty-two feels like giving up your left elbow. It's an expression of how you're different from me. Our stuff remains a part of our individuation throughout our entire life and lends to our sense of feeling safe in the world. Our safety blanket is now a couch throw or our favorite sweater.

As children get older, their sense of self becomes even more individualized through their preferences.

I want this doll.

I want this green truck.

Of course, this is also the beginning of parental and societal influences on who we *should* be in the world and therefore what items we *should* possess. Adolescence is the stage when we start to notice and question our preferences as being different from those of our caregivers.

Our innate desire toward possessing things for individuation doesn't stop in childhood. Our belongings have always been and will continue to be an integral way of expressing our identity in the world in combination with our cultural conditioning specific to our experiences.

I have the rose gold iPhone. Translation: I'm elegant and appreciate design.

I have the black Samsung phone. Translation: I'm smart and don't fall for fluff.

Possessing, owning, liking, desiring, or buying things is not the problem when it comes to clutter. The problem comes when we outgrow certain identities but keep holding on to items representing the old identity. We don't shed the old identity to make room for the inevitable new one. And since our identity is reflected through our stuff, we hang on to those items that represent the past identities. The past not only remains present, but also piles up. Think of a snake needing to shed its skin, but instead each layer continues to pile on top of the previous. The once-lithe snake is now heavy and encumbered.

Possessing, owning, liking, desiring, or buying things is not the problem when it comes to clutter. The problem comes when we outgrow certain identities but keep holding on to items representing the old identity. We don't shed the old identity to make room for the inevitable new one.

Throughout childhood, our choices are influenced, if not solely made, by our caregivers. After all, they are feeding us and taking care of us. Maintaining approval is instinctively important. Forming a sense of self is laden with parental influence, even under the most relaxed parenting styles. Our world is limited by our caregivers' filtering, not to mention our familial and cultural lenses.

As we get older, we gain more exposure to a bigger world. We also have the ability to take care of ourselves, so survival is not dependent on our caregivers, at least physically. Our likes and dislikes broaden as it becomes safer to extend beyond familial preferences and also narrow as we become more aligned to our unique stamp on the world. This isn't an overnight process. In fact, this process is our life journey as we shape-shift our way through a series of identity crises. No one is exempt from these transitional times.

Instead of crises, as they so often seem, they can be viewed as opportunities—opportunities to come into alignment with who we really are. Unfortunately, though, identity shifts also happen as a result of catalytic events, such as the sudden death of a loved one, divorce, job loss, or other unforeseen happenings. You've most likely experienced events or situations that in hindsight seem like before and after moments. Out of nowhere, life is forever changed. You are forever changed. And your identity is changed or, at least, expanded or refined.

There is a bias in our society about changing who we are. It's not usually favored among family and friends, not to mention ourselves. If we change, then those around us become threatened by it and scared that they too will have to make changes. In some cultures, changing identity can lead to persecution, if not imprisonment. Identity is a big deal and at the heart of most of our struggles on every level—personal, cultural, and societal.

There comes a time in all our lives when an identity no longer serves us. Maybe you were once known as the uncatchable catch in college. Now you are ready to settle down in a committed relationship. We have to let go of old identities that are no longer in alignment with the life we want to be living. Although our soul is always urging us forward, it's easy to hold on to the known past. The stuff we're reluctant to let go of is a direct representation.

Change is inevitably difficult. Surrendering to and accepting change is probably the hardest work we as humans face and is at the heart of most spiritual teachings. In the book *ChangeAbility: How Artists, Activists, and Awakeners Navigate Change*, author Sharon Weil discusses activating change, inspiring change, and adapting to change. Weil provides some practical ways of navigating change, particularly when change is imposed upon us. Like the art of arranging our spaces in feng shui, change should ideally meander like a winding path through our life rather than rush or stagnate. This keeps life interesting without feeling overwhelming.

Like the art of arranging our spaces
in feng shui, change should ideally
meander like a winding path through
our life rather than rush or stagnate.
This keeps life interesting without feeling
overwhelming.

Change is essential for our evolution and expansion. Sometimes change happens in small increments that we hardly even notice, and other times we feel like we've been sucker punched out of nowhere. Either way, we go through periods of time when it feels like our identity is up for grabs. We have no idea who we are. The person we thought we were is no longer. Rest assured, though, that it's a part of our natural evolution of being human. With more understanding and normalizing of these critical times in our life, change can be met with more ease, grace, and compassion for oneself.

Your home reveals how well you flow with or resist change. For example, if you have outdated interiors that lack your own personal expression, you may be resisting change. When I go into a client's home, I can immediately spot outdated items that do not fit with the individual, from couches, to artwork, to simple decor items sitting around. For others, past identities are tucked away in closets or other storage areas. In either case, the issue is deeper than the stuff.

What identities are you holding on to past their expiration date? The ego will hold on to identities with a death grip. The term *ego* was made popular through the work of psychoanalyst Sigmund Freud in the early 1920s. Since then, there have been many opinions and theories, from spiritual teachers to psychologists, on whether the ego is friend, foe, or a combination.

It's generally agreed upon, however, that the ego is that aspect of us that governs our rational thinking and equips us for basic survival.

This includes our personality—that which separates us from others, or, in other words, our identity. It also comes with defense mechanisms that keep us seeking short-term pleasure in lieu of experiencing acute pain or even grief.

The ego keeps us safe and is necessary for navigating life in the physical realm. But the ego doesn't like change. Change is the unknown and unpredictable world where our identity could be lost. When we meet change with resistance, we stop the flow of our life. Resistance puts the brakes on possible changes we don't want in addition to changes we might want. Change forces the ego to meet its match and perhaps even face its demise.

When Ego Meets Change

Although the ego has been the driving force behind our psyche, it's only one component of who we are. Yes, we are here having a human experience, but we are also spiritual beings. Being *human* and a *being* is a constant navigation of the physical and spiritual worlds. If the ego is *self* with a little *s*, our soul is *Self* with a capital *S*.

We are waking up to the realization that we are more than our physical body being driven by an ego that is only out for itself. We also have an eternal soul within our physical shell with a constant connection to God, the universe, or Source energy that is here, not only for seeking physical pleasures for our self, but also for growth and expansion of our Self.

With the rapid evolution of mental, emotional, and spiritual aspects of ourselves, the presence of our Self is becoming more palpable in our everyday life. Although a vast hierarchy of needs still exists on the planet, our problems are evolving from running from the saber-toothed tiger to fulfilling our life purpose. This is true in relationships too. Our relationships are evolving from those based on survival needs to those based upon compatibility and fulfillment of purpose. ✒

The collective is moving toward transcending our ego-driven one-dimensionality to more spiritual living. Currently, however, we are caught in between these two paradigms. This makes it particularly challenging to strike a balance between our ego self trying to survive in a physical body with our spiritual Self seeking expansion. This is why the self-help industry has exploded in recent years.

In addition to the our spiritual expansion, we are also living longer than previous generations. When you put these two factors together, we are essentially living multiple lives within one lifetime. Instead of going through the full motions of physically dying and being reborn, we are instead shedding our ego and evolving into new personalities, or identities, all within one lifetime. Instead of a physical death, we experience the death of our ego, or identity.

The end of the ego as one knows it is nothing new to the human condition. Commonly referred to as the *dark night of the soul*, it can be traced to biblical times and is now used in Jungian psychology. Thomas Moore, author of *Dark Nights of the Soul*, sees this time as a rite of passage, or a transitory period that we go through in life. In nature, it's most akin to the caterpillar transforming into the butterfly.

The ego doesn't go down without a fight. Transitioning from living a life as a corporate manager to a holistic health coach comes with a lot of confusion, as does leaving a marriage and three children. It's as if we're suddenly thrown into situations that have no owner's manual on how to proceed or what to do next. How to integrate two different worlds seems next to impossible. And it usually is. There is a dark gap in between the world we leave and the world we enter. This gap time is the dark night of the soul.

These changes come with a tremendous amount of social and familial pressures, leaving us dissatisfied with the past and fearful of the future.

I know who I used to be. I know who I want to be. But who am I now? And what cost will I have to pay to go from my past self to my future self? What will I have to give up and will it be worth it?

These are the conversations we have with ourselves, consciously or unconsciously. The ego will always opt for comfort, the known, while the soul will always go toward expansion, the unknown. There lies the push-pull alive within all of us.

To make the process even more gut-wrenching, our family, our friends, and society often don't want us to change either. But with more awareness, the process doesn't have to be so drenched in fear and struggle. As soon as you become aware of what's really at the heart of the internal struggle, then you can ease into the transition. This is where working with your home can be such a valuable tool to see what's really going on. Whatever identity you're trying to hold on to is in your home in the form of clutter. It's those items you wrestle with each time you come around to decluttering.

So often the pain is in what we make something mean rather than the actual event itself that creates suffering. For example, if a relationship ends and you make it mean that you've been rejected or that you'll grow old and alone, therein lies the greatest suffering. Peace can actually be attained during these times if fully embraced. After all, peace is found in the transcendence of judging something to be good or bad. We all have encountered and will continue to encounter challenging times in our lives, but by rising above the stories there is an opportunity to find peace while also experiencing the emotions of these difficult times.

The Hero's Journey to Rediscover Your Soul

Seeing a bigger picture of where you are in your own journey is helpful in getting perspective in times of change. The hero's journey is the closest to a formula we have for the typical stages we face in times of immense change in our personal lives. It's no wonder that the hero's journey has been and continues to be the basic formula for most Hollywood storytelling. Joseph Campbell first coined the term *hero's journey* in his 1949 book *The Hero with a Thousand Faces*. In short, the hero's journey is a myth in which the hero goes on an adventure, faces a crisis, and comes back home transformed as a result. If this sounds like the basis of every story and movie you've ever read or seen, it's because it is. The journey of Dorothy in *The Wizard of Oz* is a classic example.

The basis of the hero's journey is a mirror of the human condition and why we relate so much to these classic stories. It's a transformational formula that is part of our collective consciousness and, in essence, the journey from an old identity to a new identity. While the details of our own stories are unique, we are all traveling through the same journey. The climactic point of the hero's journey is the dark night of the soul. For those who have been through a dark night, you may be of the belief that a physical death would actually be easier. The ego hangs on with a vice grip and you truly feel like you are dying while awake. It is the ultimate grief—the grief of your old self.

By simply being born, you embarked upon the ultimate hero's journey. Within this journey of life are a series of mini journeys. At all times you are engaged in one of the stages of the journey. Which one and for how long is the only variable. This is based upon your astrology, your soul's plan, and your free will. The hero's journey is ultimately for the purpose of expansion, and expansion of your soul is the purpose for coming into this life experience.

The hero's journey has been characterized in stories that date back thousands of years, from the *The Odyssey* to *Moby Dick* to *Forrest Gump*. It has been a story archetype in religions and virtually every Hollywood story. Why, then, are we so surprised when it happens to us? Why do we think we are so alone? Well, actually, you are alone.

And that's the point. The hero's journey is a solo journey. You may have the same people in your life while going through it, but you will feel alone in your trials and tribulations.

In movies, it's usually men who embark upon the hero's journey. The journey of men is usually an outward conflict, and with women it's often an internal struggle. But we are all subject to the fate of the journey. It's been a part of our collective consciousness since the beginning of storytelling and will continue to be until a new way of expansion evolves for the collective.

The hero's journey is a quantum leap into a new life path that is necessary for your continuation in this incarnation. When you have expanded as far as you can in your current life situation, the hero's journey will beckon to you. For most people, this will be the death of the ego, or the death of an identity that is no longer serving your expansion. It is releasing your old world for a new world. The hardest part is that you don't know what the new one is going to be. Faith is your only ally.

Like the caterpillar becoming the butterfly, the hero's journey is an alchemical transformation that calls for growing pains. The amount of spiritual healing during this period can be deep and profound. However, this intensity is necessary to ultimately transform old patterns and belief systems inherited from previous generations that are no longer desired so that you can live authentically to your soul's highest calling.

The biggest tragedy of your life would be to deny your greatest destiny for the sake of mediocrity.

The hero's journey is a wake-up call that you have pre-agreed to, and yet free will is always at play. The biggest tragedy of your life would be to deny your greatest destiny for the sake of mediocrity. The hero's journey is the Divine via your higher self stepping in to get you on your highest path—the path to your heart.

Discovering who you are is often an essential part of the hero's journey. You release the influence of those around you to realize what your preferences really are. You become your own science project of what piques your interest, independent of others in your life. Most of us have bent to the whims of others most of our life. This is how we have been socialized. The hero's journey is a course correction to get you back to the path of your heart.

Before I knew about the hero's journey or that I was about to step into my own, I had a dream that I later realized foreshadowed my hero's journey. I was walking in the woods with a group of people. We had been on a long camping trip. As you would see in a movie, we were coming to the end of the trip with even a rainbow in the vista. Everyone was relieved to see that we had arrived. And then right at that moment I realized my dog, Horatia, was not with me. Horatia was my dog who passed in 2011. She is a personal dream symbol that represents my heart.

In the dream I realized she was lost in the woods. There was no question that I had to go back and find her. And so I turned from the group and went into the woods on a long solo journey to find her. And I did. I will never forget how it felt when she ran into my arms. Interestingly, that was not the end of the dream. I was not out of the woods yet. True to all hero's journeys, I still had to endure the final test before I woke up.

The ultimate point of the hero's journey
is the journey back to you—
back to your heart.

The ultimate point of the hero's journey is the journey back to you—back to your heart. It's not about finding the perfect career, perfect soul mate, or perfect geographical location. Those are the byproducts of living in alignment with you. It's reuniting and living from your heart, the one you abandoned so long ago without realizing it.

The hero's journey is inherently lonely. But knowing where you are on the path can be helpful in realizing that even in your aloneness, you're not alone. The following sections consolidate the twelve steps of the hero's journey into three primary steps: refusal of the call, the dark night, and the final test.

Refusal of the Call

Very few volunteer for a hero's journey, at least consciously. It's oftentimes a crisis that tips the first domino. In the *Wizard of Oz*, Dorothy attempted to first leave on her own but was persuaded to return. Instead, it took a crisis—a tornado—for her to finally answer the call.

What call did you refuse before the tornado? It was probably some rumbling of thunder in the distance that you simply brushed aside as no big deal. Maybe the thunder got closer. And louder. Eventually, it can no longer be ignored. It's best to address the call for change before it gets to a crisis point. When we live in denial or in resistance to change, we are more likely to get blindsided. For example, you find out you've been cheated on for two years. The stressful job is now causing high blood pressure. Or the fear of leaving an unhealthy relationship leads to the need for depression medication.

Generally, people only change through pain or pleasure. Unfortunately, it's usually pain because we find too much guilt in following the pleasure, hence the often-used term *guilty pleasure*. With pain, we earn our stripes and it makes us believe that maybe we are deserving of something good. An intuitive once told me, "You keep choosing heartbreak to get in touch with your heart." It doesn't have to be that way for me or you. Pain or suffering has been the most common path to awakening the soul, mainly because it was the layers of pain that we packed on over many generations that must be undone to reach the core of who we are.

Most people are not willing to step onto hot burning coals, and, therefore, it usually takes a catalytic person or event to put us in the throes of the fire. And then we are left wondering *Why is this happening to me?* when, really, there were signs along the way. We always think we're the exception to the rule until life happens to us. You hear stories but never think they will happen to you. These difficult times call up existential questions that are not easily answered.

Why am I here?

What's the purpose of life anyway?

What is my purpose in life?

What should I do with my life?

Inherent to a quest is a question. A quest involves experiences to find the answers and is not for the faint of heart. By the end of your journey, you will have a new understanding of who you are, your place in the world, and what you are here to do. And if you don't, you'll be basking in enough joy to not really care and realize that that really is the point.

Like Dorothy, most of us are reluctant to leave "home." Home is where our comforts are. This is usually why we are reluctant to answer the call. We refuse to leave our comfort zone. And it is our comfort zone from which our soul is trying to shake us. Our comfort zone is safe. Safe is what's familiar, and what's unfamiliar is usually where our fears lie. Even though your ego self seeks safety and security, your soul says otherwise. The larger the gap between your ego and your soul, the unhappier you will be. As you begin to close this gap, you will feel more and more in alignment with your true and authentic self. The soul will eventually win out and you will answer the call.

The Dark Night

In Hollywood screenwriting, act 2 is where most of the action takes place and is the longest of the three acts. As a screenwriter, you are to put your character through every obstacle you can think of. And so is the case with our own hero's journey. After you answer the call to begin the journey, you will face challenge after challenge after challenge. By now, there is no turning back. There is nothing behind you but the open sea, and everything you have learned now comes into play. None of your old tricks work. You run out of distractions and your old comforts are no longer comfortable.

When challenges arise, it's easy to slip into feeling like a victim of circumstances. This is part of the healing process. Any wounding caused by victimhood or martyrdom will be put under a microscope to heal and transform. The hero must die in order to be reborn. Your biggest fears must be faced and transformed. When you begin to wonder *Who am I?* is when you know the process is working. Having an identity crisis is an inevitable part and, in some cases, the ultimate point of the hero's journey. It is the death of the ego as you've known it.

We think of an identity crisis as not
knowing who we are, but it's really
the soul's cry for becoming whole.

We think of an identity crisis as not knowing who we are, but it's really the soul's cry for becoming whole. It's becoming 100 percent of who you really are by reclaiming all the pieces and parts that were abandoned over the years. These are our shadow sides that we hid from ourselves and others long ago. We are on a journey to retrieve those aspects and integrate them. Meanwhile, we are releasing personas, or subpersonalities, we picked up along the way for the purpose of gaining approval and consequentially surviving our early formative years.

Through this process, you will discover new aspects of yourself that you didn't know existed. For example, you may be more artistically inclined than you thought. Or perhaps you have spiritual gifts you weren't aware of and are only now open enough to receive. These are parts of yourself that weren't safe enough, cool enough, or accepted enough for you to fully embrace. And so you abandoned them. Reclaiming these shadow aspects of ourselves is at the heart of the hero's journey.

During the dark night phase of my journey, I found myself very alone and desiring a partner. I resented the universe for withholding this from me. But I realized that while there were some legitimate reasons for wanting someone in my life, there were also unhealthy aspects of desiring a relationship that needed to heal, such as the feeling of lacking completion, the fear of being alone or abandoned, and the need to fill other void aspects of myself.

The dark night was like chemo treatments: in killing the bad cells, the good cells are killed off too. I had to be withheld from the good, healthy aspects of partnership in order to heal the toxic aspects. And it was those toxic aspects that had, in fact, led to the demise of all my former relationships. I realized that the dark night was not a curse, but a gift to redeem me of future grievances in relationships and to set me up for a relationship not based upon need, but unconditional love. The dark night was the answer to my prayers and the object of all my manifesting.

During this time, my intuition became heightened in the form of signs, symbols, and dreams. Synchronicities showed up that could not be denied. They were nothing short of miraculous and could only be explained with divine intervention. This was a welcome relief following a time in which I couldn't trust myself to change a light bulb. Common to the hero's journey is a newfound trust of self. Our friends, teachers, and mentors can only help us to a certain extent. As a result, self-trust, self-validation, and self-acknowledgment begin to emerge. And then when you think you're out of the woods, the new and improved version of yourself is put to a final test.

The Final Test

In Hollywood thrillers, just when the bad guy has been slain and you can almost put your popcorn down, he comes back for one final blow. With just enough breath to cause the hero to sweat, the nemesis wields the knife with a final, but futile, attempt to take down the hero. I use the word *futile* because we know by this point that the hero will win. And so do you. You know you'll come out alive at this point of your journey. You've been through too much not to. And yet, you will question everything, one last time. This is the final test stage of the hero's journey.

Why is the final test necessary? Its purpose is integration before you can finally move into your new world with all the new wisdom fully intact. We all think we can skip steps on the hero's journey, especially this one. After coming out of the dark night still alive, you think, *What else could possibly happen?* You are ready to begin living your new life. Deservedly so, right? However, to fully immerse yourself in your new life everything you have gained must be fully integrated.

At this point of my journey, I had faced many dark nights square in the face (read: in the fetal position). I was starting to vision my new future and even had hindsight around what I had gone through. I was actually enjoying being by myself. I was feeling at home in Los Angeles (which is not an easy feat for anyone). I was excited about embracing life again and fully living. I set intentions for what 2016 would bring—after all, it had to be good. Those were just the odds. The wheel of fortune had to turn in my favor.

And then on December 31, 2015, the unthinkable happened. My mom was diagnosed with terminal leukemia. She had her first chemo treatment on January 1, 2016, her seventy-sixth birthday. Cancer always comes as a shock, but this was particularly shocking for someone who rarely gets sick and was playing tennis four days a week just a couple of months prior. My mom was the strongest-willed person I'd ever known, a true Capricorn. How could this happen?

With memories of all the times she had taken care of me, from strep throat to pulled wisdom teeth to facial reconstructive surgery, I knew I needed to be there to help take care of her. Because she had a prognosis of three to ten months, each moment with her would be a gift. I knew what I needed to do. I flew to LA, terminated my lease, put everything into storage, and flew back to Nashville as fast as I could. Three days later, she died. I was now motherless, homeless, and back in the same city I had worked so hard to move from.

In cycling through a spectrum of emotions, from victimhood to unconditional love, I had to trust my decision that temporarily moving back was the right thing to do. I realized that I had had multiple prophetic dreams a few months prior that foretold these events. It gave me comfort that all of this was predestined in some way and there was some order to the chaos. I could resist or surrender. I did both. I resisted during most of the cold and rainy month of February. I surrendered in March.

In addition to grieving and helping with family logistics, I was evidently back in my hometown to resolve anything unresolved. All was up for review, from college friendships to past relationships to my relationship with my mom. Turns out, the evidence of all of this was sitting in my closet to sift through and purge. In doing so, I was able to reclaim lost aspects of myself and integrate the benefits of the work I had endured through the previous stages of my journey.

Even up to the time of writing this book, I was integrating the events of early 2016 and completing what felt like a three-year journey within a decade-long hero's journey.

With the twists and turns that life brings, it's sometimes hard to keep up with where we are on our journey. But we are all somewhere on the hero's journey at all times. These plot twists are actually written and predetermined stages of life that we all go through. How we fill in the script is determined by our free will. Or maybe free will is just our resistance to our destiny.

A hero's journey forever changes you. Your beliefs, desires, life purpose, geographical location, and sometimes even physical appearance transform as you become a new version of yourself. You may have a sudden desire to purge old clothing, redecorate, or move altogether. If so, go with this natural inclination. Our home environment is an external projection of our internal self and, thus, the desire to release items related to the old identity is a common response to the hero's journey.

Resistance to this natural shedding can prolong the stages of the journey, or it could be a desired pause in order to travel at a manageable pace. With more awareness about the purpose of these life-changing times, we can experience them as breakthroughs instead of breakdowns. That being said, pain is inevitable at certain points of our journey.

Ultimately, life is full of ups and downs, many of which we have little if any control over. We have choice during a hero's journey, unlike when we experience sudden catalytic events that come out of nowhere and dramatically change us.

Catalytic Events That Shape Us

You've most likely experienced one or more events in your life that forever changed you. They feel completely out of the blue and you are never the same again. These major changes are oftentimes the result of a catalytic event. You can see this on the world stage as well.

Tragedy opens our hearts in ways that weren't accessible prior to the event. The human spirit is touched during tragic events as we rush to help in any way possible, such as donating money, giving blood, sending prayers, or shedding a tear for complete strangers. When this happens on a more personal level, it is especially life changing.

During the few weeks I spent with my mom in the hospital as she withered away at a pace my mind couldn't comprehend, my heart was broken open. While experiencing the most tragic event up to that point in my life, I was also thrust into a massive heart awakening. While I was experiencing this, one of my best friends was in the process of falling in love. In comparing notes about our day, we were actually in complete vibrational alignment. Both of us were experiencing a heart expansion through love, just flip sides of the same coin.

As difficult as that experience was, as was my divorce, career change, and major move, I was changed for the better. These are the events that occur in our lives that illicit an identity crisis. We are forever changed as a result. Catalytic events usually happen outside our control, or at least it feels that way. You can come out the other side either softer or harder. You can play victim and blame God and others or you can surrender to something bigger than yourself.

In any event, it takes time to integrate these changes and start anew. It has been well documented that these are the most stressful times in our life:

- Death of a loved one
- Divorce
- Move
- Major illness
- Job loss

These events leave us with no sense of grounding and have us questioning everything. It can take years to recover and regain a new sense of self. Catalytic events are often followed by a period of shock.

It is advisable to make as few decisions as possible during this time. The mind is in survival mode and not capable of making higher-level or longer-term decisions. The Zen saying "chop wood, carry water" is appropriate during this time when even basic tasks, such as sleeping and eating, can be challenging.

Depending on the severity of the event, it may be recommended to work with a therapist, energy healer, or mental health professional, especially if trauma is stored in the body. It is important to release any held energy and emotions from the body for optimal mental and physical health.

When it comes time to decluttering items related to these difficult times, an extra dose of time and compassion should be given to yourself or others going through the process. Chapter 6 discusses the grief process in detail and can assist you in letting go of items associated with loss.

When emotions surrounding changes in our life are not fully dealt with over time, it's easy to stay stuck in that time. Evidence of these unprocessed emotions shows up in our homes, closets, and office spaces. These are the items that keep us stuck. This is when a clutter intervention is needed. In the following chapters, starting with items from relationships, you will start to identify those items that can move you from the past to the present and into your ideal future.

CHAPTER 3

Stuck on You

Past Relationships

Relationships are the area of our life in which we are most prone to losing ourselves, while in them and also after they've ended. Romantic relationships are close-up mirrors in which the lines of where I end and you begin become blurred. For this reason, it's easy to lose our sense of self. When this happens, it's because our own identity was never firmly in place to begin with and, as a result, we become a chameleon to the person with whom we're in relationship. Of course, this is also the reason why many relationships fail. We blame the other person for losing ourselves in the relationship.

When relationships end, we are left with the remnants of the relationship, from shared furniture to exchanged gifts to photos. Because our energy was so interweaved with the other's energy, getting rid of those items can feel like a ripping of one's soul. That's because it is. The energy field between two people, particularly in long-term relationships, takes time to unwind. Of course, this also makes it that much more imperative that items related to that past relationship be let go, when the time is right, in order to move on.

People seeking a relationship often question why they haven't attracted a partner. In most cases, it's because there hasn't been a proper letting go of a former relationship. There is only so much space in our heart, our emotions, our energy field, and our home. If there is lingering energy from a previous relationship, it will prevent a new one from coming in.

In cases where there is a quick turn-around in relationships, or perhaps even an overlap, the new relationship will be of the same vibration as the former one. In other words, it will be virtually the same person with the same issues replaying themselves like a recording.

One of the best ways to clear
out past relationships is to clear out
items related to them.

One of the best ways to clear out past relationships is to clear out items related to them. Leftover items with a strong reminder of the previous relationship are physical manifestations of the underlying energy of the relationship. As you let go of the items, you let go of aspects of the relationship until nothing is left between you. This is scary for most people and something they're not willing to do. There is a fear of completely letting someone go, especially someone who loved and adored you. This is especially true if there's lingering hope of that person coming back. However, a clean slate will provide a space for someone even better to come in.

Committed relationships are a tall order—we're asked to merge our energy, our resources, and our lives together for the best chances of success. And then if things don't work out, we're forced to un-

tangle the energy and become independent, sovereign beings chart-
ing off onto a new course. This is a fearful predicament leaving many
with one foot in and one foot out of relationships in an attempt to
preserve their individuality or avoid complete abandonment by the
other person. Unfortunately, the lack of commitment often leads to
the actual thing one is trying to avoid.

> The degree to which the couple's
> possessions are merged
> is the same proportion to which
> their energies have merged.

The degree to which the couple's possessions are merged is the
same proportion to which their energies have merged. For example, are the books integrated on the bookshelf, or does each person
have their own bookshelf? Neither is right or wrong. It depends on
the preferences of the couple. One approach is to have a balance of
merged spaces and individualized spaces. This represents each person maintaining their individual expression with the relationship being the third entity.

When a relationship ends, it can be difficult to know what to do
with shared items and those related to the relationship in some way,
whether functional or sentimental. For some couples the physical
items are not important, whereas for others they become bargaining chips for unresolved angst toward one another. Even after the co-
owned items have been divvied up or sold, it can take years to sift
through the emotions held by leftover items from the relationship.

Even in relationships where there was harmonious agreement
over items, the individual exploration of whether to hold on to certain items is a process that can linger for years. This is part of the

healing process of fully letting go of the relationship in some way. The reluctance to let go may not always be about the other person per se, but about letting go of some aspect that the relationship represented.

Even in relationships in which there was harmonious agreement over items, the individual exploration of whether to hold on to certain items is a process that can linger for years.

Inherent to grieving a relationship is grieving the former identity one held while in the relationship. Our identity in a relationship can come in the form of social opportunities, cultural acceptance, family relations, hobbies, and even in changing our name. When the relationship ends, we are left wondering who we are.

Who am I without this other person, without a partner, without my other half?

Formulating a new sense of self, or identity, is not an overnight process and is perhaps part of the hero's journey of finding one's true Self as separate from another person. To avoid this trepid exploration, some people may opt for a replacement as soon as possible to not feel the loss of identity. This is commonly referred to as a *rebound* relationship and used to soften the landing. This usually leads to the same patterns of the former relationship, the success of which will depend on the level of self-inquiry and healing that has taken place.

After a breakup or divorce, if one of the parties remains in the shared home, it will be much harder for that person to move on.

Spaces hold patterns and memories of everything that has happened there. To create a new life in the same space is not impossible, but it is challenging. The person more resistant to change, particularly as it relates to the ending of the relationship, will oftentimes end up staying in the home. However, if financially feasible, it would be ideal if both parties moved to a new home in order to move forward and start fresh.

> Spaces hold patterns and memories of everything that has happened there. To create a new life in the same space is not impossible, but it is challenging.

The 2008 to 2010 housing market crash created unusual situations in which separated or divorced couples were forced to stay living together because they couldn't afford to move from the house. It would be interesting to know the percentage of couples who ended up staying together as a result compared to those who jumped ship as soon as the market corrected.

The number of physical items that result from a dissolved relationship varies depending on the length of the relationship. For example, couples that cohabitated have more merged belongings to sort out than those with a casual dating experience. In either case, there are memories, hopes, and disappointments that have to be cleared, which are all memorialized by items, from silverware to Instagram photos. The following sections will give insight on how to deal with shared items, gifts received from the other person, mementos, and photos from past relationships.

Shared Items

Breakups, divorces, and death of a loved one are filled with emotional anguish. The hopes, the dreams, and the visions, in addition to the good and bad memories, all have to be washed away or at least properly stored. Your entire life has to be reframed, literally and figuratively. The last thing you want to deal with is the stuff—the physical belongings you shared. It seems trivial in the big picture and yet it's anything but. The physical items are a representation of the relationship.

Financial distress often follows a divorce and only adds to the emotional impact and logistics around shared items. Having to adjust from shared expenses to individual expenses complicates the ability to move forward. While starting over with a brand-new bedroom suite sounds great, it may not be feasible to do so.

The approach to divvying out shared items differs among couples, which is usually a mirror of the relationships. For some couples, it's a pragmatic approach, whereas for others it ends up as an explosive exchange that drags out for months, if not years. The process is a mirror of the conflict resolution behaviors in the relationship. If it was a heated, turbulent relationship, don't expect the breakup to be any different. Or, if the relationship lacked passion and ran more like a business, then expect the split of assets to be similar.

The possessions we come into a relationship with represent our individual identity separate from the relationship. Items acquired during the relationship, particularly those purchased jointly, represent one's identity as it pertains to the relationship. It is those items that are more difficult and require a clutter intervention.

In *The Life-Changing Magic of Tidying Up*, Marie Kondo suggests asking, "Does it spark joy?" in determining whether to keep something or not. This is a great standard, but it can be tricky when applied to items that hold conflicting emotions mixed with pragmatic implications.

Having a sofa to sit on brings me joy, but thinking about my ex every time I sit down doesn't so much. Kicking back on the gorgeous linen sofa I picked out from Restoration Hardware brings me joy, but remembering the arguments we've had on the couch doesn't bring me joy. Sitting on the floor of my empty apartment definitely doesn't spark joy.

We prefer a bright-line rule in determining what to keep and what not to keep from a prior relationship; however, each item and each person is different. Keep in mind that what seems practical to keep could end up costing too much in its emotional weight. I had one client who kept putting off replacing her couch from her prior relationship. Even though she could afford a new couch, it didn't seem practical to do so. Her relationship with her ex was unpleasant, and the couch subconsciously reminded her on a daily basis of that relationship, which diminished her energy.

Your energy is your most valuable asset—it's what attracts new people, new money, and new opportunities into your life. How you feel, especially in your home, is vital to manifesting what you want in your life. Any negativity that has not been worked through and processed from a relationship will be held within associated items. For example, if you felt belittled and powerless in the relationship with your ex, then items pertaining to the relationship will affect you similarly on a subconscious level.

Any negativity that has not been
worked through and processed
from a relationship will be held
within associated items.

Also be conscious of whether the shared items feel representative of who you are now. When we go through a divorce or breakup, it usually comes with a major shift in identity. Who you were in the relationship may be different from who you are on the other side of it. When I went through a divorce, I was living in a new-construction home in the suburbs and then moved to an urban neighborhood in a Craftsman-style home that felt much more like me. The pickled oak dining room set that came with me, on the other hand, did not feel like me. It was clear that it needed to go even if it meant the dining room would be empty for a while.

If you decide to keep certain shared items, I recommend space clearing them. Just like a room can be cleared of negative or stagnant energy, furniture or any physical item can also be energy cleared. Burning a sage bundle and wafting it around furniture items with the intention of clearing previously held energy is a common method of space clearing. A more in-depth explanation of space clearing techniques can be found in my book *Mind, Body, Home*. With sage smudging you can clear away the previous energy that the item holds in its energy field. This can help give you a fresh start and peace of mind.

That being said, you may continue to associate specific memories with certain items despite the best space-clearing attempts. If this feels true for you, then consider getting rid of the item. A shared bed is a common example of this. The memories we hold around a shared bed in a relationship are often strong, hard to erase, and usually beyond the benefits of space clearing.

When decluttering items from a past relationship, the most important thing to remember is to be extremely compassionate with yourself during the process. Splitting from another person is a literal splitting of energy fields that must be done gradually to avoid shock. In cases where there was an abrupt split, dealing with the leftover items gradually can be a way to process the breakup in your own time. This is where decluttering can be a cathartic healing process.

> When the other person is no longer
> available for closure, it is through our
> stuff that the grief process can occur
> and release can happen for final
> completion of the relationship.

When the other person is no longer available for closure, it is through our stuff that the grief process can occur and release can happen for final completion of the relationship. Letting go of a relationship is no different from grieving a death. It's crucial to allow the grief process to unfold so as to not harbor regret and resentment later on. Chapter 6 gives a more detailed examination of the grief process.

Gifts Received

The expression and exchange of love is often represented through gifts. In fact, receiving gifts is one of the five "love languages" in Gary Chapman's popular relationship book, *The 5 Love Languages*. Unfortunately, when relationships end, knowing what to do with those once-precious gifts can be an excruciating process as the sweetness turns to sorrow.

Deciding what to do with gifts received once the relationship has ended is a difficult process. Again, there is no right or wrong answer and, in fact, your decision may shift over time. This is representative of how time heals and is a mirror of the healing process. Immediately getting rid of all the gifts received can feel too sudden and harsh, unless done out of anger. With more time for processing, understanding, and perspective, a gift that once held a special place in your heart is replaced with new experiences and memories. What once seemed like a priceless Valentine's Day card may later seem like ancient history.

Some gifts are so specific to the person and situation in which they were given that it's impossible to separate them. An engagement ring is the most obvious example. Other gifts, on the other hand, may not hold an emotional charge with the relationship. When you look at the item, do you first think about the person who gave it to you or the item itself? I have gifts from past relationships that, while I remember who gave them to me, I don't associate with that person. The item has become so much a part of me as opposed to an association with the relationship.

Another factor is the terms you are on with this person. Is the relationship tenuous, or combustible? Are you not talking, cordial co-parents, or best friends? The role and the emotions this person plays in your life now are important considerations in deciding what to do with gifts. For relationships in which there continue to be strong irreconcilable differences, I don't recommend keeping gifts that were received. Even if things are ironed out later down the road, letting go of the exchanges that took place during the relationship will most likely be necessary to arrive at a peaceful place.

For relationships in which you are now friends, the emotional charge around gifts may not be as strong. However, be mindful that your continued relationship with this person isn't serving as an emotional crutch preventing a new love from coming in. If this is the case, consider releasing some of the gifts that represent your past relationship to create space for new gifts to be exchanged in a new relationship.

Mementos

It's often the little things in relationships that mean the most. These are represented through cards, movie tickets, or any other type of memento. As a nostalgic Cancer sign and hopeless romantic, I'm a sucker for these otherwise inconsequential items. Unlike gifts, mementos usually have little, if any, monetary value and are instead rich in memories. They are a minefield of emotions and therefore ripe for releasing the past.

I had one client who hired me to help feng shui her home after her ex moved out. Still written on the bathroom mirror was "I Love You" in red lipstick. It's the mementos that can be the hardest to let go of and yet the most powerful to do so for moving forward. Unlike gifts, for which there can be practical value in keeping the item beyond the relationship, mementos are solely about the relationship.

These precious items should be handled with compassion, as they are at the heart of the grieving process. If you are still hanging on to such items from past relationships from long ago, consider why you are still holding on to them and if now is the time to let them go. Even if you are in a new relationship, hanging on to items from a past relationship can represent an emotional tie to the former person, even if they are no longer in your life. What have you not let go of from that relationship? The energy between two people can still be active even if there's no longer physical contact. Mementos, as well as gifts, represent an active energy cord.

Even if you are in a new relationship, hanging on to items from a past relationship can represent an emotional tie to the former person, even if they are no longer in your life.

When you are ready to come face-to-face with these items, be present to the emotions that rise up. Allow any emotions to surface and feel them, and they will then wash away and be cleared. At that point, you will have more clarity about whether it's time to release the item or not. If more healing from the relationship is needed, then you may be compelled to keep the item. Otherwise, you will be able to release the item with ease after the emotions have been felt.

Some may desire a ritualized process. Because the process of letting go is so much about healing, it may be helpful to do it in tandem with a ritual or ceremonial process. You may find a burning ceremony helpful or even using the item as part of a therapy session. In *Clearing Clutter*, author Alexandra Chauran provides several rituals to assist the process of letting go of items. Otherwise, simply say thank you and goodbye as you release an item for gratitude and closure.

Photos

What to do with photos from past loves is another tricky area to navigate. On one hand, you don't want to completely erase your past as if it never happened, and yet there is also a desire to move on and create new memories. Finding this balance is an intricate and individualized process. The energy of a particular moment is captured and held in each photo. Photos displayed, stored away in the attic, or held on a digital device are all active in your vibration. The only difference is whether that memory, or energy, is in your conscious awareness or stored away in your subconscious mind.

How we keep photos has changed dramatically over the last decade. Current generations are caught between printed photos from the past and digitally stored photos of the present. Photo albums and scrapbooks have been replaced with computer files, the cloud, and digital photo feeds. That means we have many more places to store old memories.

Whether printed or in digital format, it's difficult to know what to do with these memories. Do we just toss them or press delete? It's a stressful predicament that brings up a lot of emotion and why most people just ignore dealing with the photos altogether. In many cases, photos just get passed down for generations out of a resistance to dealing with them. This is also the same with family patterns that get passed on with each generation as well.

In his book *It Didn't Start With You*, author Mark Wolynn provides data showing how our emotional issues, which can eventually lead to physical disease, start with our ancestors. The buck stops with your generation. Don't pass your unresolved emotions down your family line. Sort through your photos and only keep the ones rich in positive and relevant memories.

Like mementos, photos have no intrinsic value. They are simply steeped in memories and emotions. There are no practical considerations for them as there are for gifts or shared items. Because there are few, if any, practical reasons for keeping photos, we know deep down we should probably get rid of them. However, the emotional implications are too high and we are likely to abandon the decluttering project altogether.

Photos push emotional triggers more so than any other items. A photo can take you back to a memory so poignantly. Photos with people pictured hold particularly powerful energy. When working with clients in their home, I pay attention to displayed photos with people, in addition to any portraiture art. Photos or artwork of people take on the energy of whoever is being depicted.

It's important that the people pictured represent positive and supportive relationships to you, whether the people are living or deceased. Think of keeping photos around like having those people actually in your home and sitting on your couch or having them over for dinner. This is especially true for pictures in your bedroom. Who do you want in this private space? In feng shui, it's a no-no to have photos of relatives and even your children in the master bedroom. The bedroom is a sacred space for just you or you and your love. Needless to say, pictures of exes are also a big no-no in the bedroom.

We often keep photos out of some obligation, as if we need an archive of our past. Is relying on our memory not enough? Or is it that we want to keep around proof that we were married, that we were in relationship with a hot person, or evidence of a life that appeared secure? Is it proof for ourselves or others? When I recently looked back on college photos that made a few round of cuts, I noticed I had been keeping the pictures of me with the cutest guys I dated. When I think about this, it's quite comical. Most of the people in the pictures now mean nothing to me, and yet I still had them tucked away in a closet like they were a jury proving that I was desirable.

Who are you allowing to take up space in your energy field? Just take a look at your photos. Pictures of exes should be kept to a minimum, if kept at all. Wedding photos following a divorce are particularly difficult to determine whether or not to keep. The difficulty in parting with our stuff is always proportional to the emotions attached. Added to the equation are the heightened emotions of the wedding day, not to mention the price tag spent for making it special.

In determining whether the wedding photos should stay or go, listen to your inner dialogue about getting rid of them.

What a shame to throw them away.

What a complete waste.

I'm at a loss about what to do with all these pictures.

Your own words hold clues to what emotions are still associated with the photos and therefore the relationship. *Shame. Waste. Loss.* When you realize what emotions about the dissolved marriage are still active, you will have more clarity in your decision to keep the wedding album or not.

For photos and mementos, don't feel like it has to be an all-or-nothing process, unless that's what feels right for you. Instead, it could be a gradual process over time. I was able to get rid of my wedding album, save for a few of my favorite pictures. Years later, I tossed all of them except for one or two to keep for personal history. At some point, perhaps those will go too. That has been a process that has worked for me regarding photos from all past significant relationships.

Dealing with items from the past, particularly past relationships, is never fun. Neither is going to therapy, but we do it because we end up feeling better afterward. Decluttering the past is a powerfully transformational process. It is more than a methodical process of getting rid of tangible items. It's a deep energy clearing of stored emotions that are held within your mind and body. Processing the past through items that represent those emotions is an invaluable healing process. Don't underestimate the energy you are shifting. Always approach the process with compassion for yourself.

At any point while decluttering emotion-filled items, if you don't feel comfortable letting something go, then don't. This simply means it's not time yet. This may be contrary advice to other decluttering books. Getting rid of an item before you've processed the energy around it is a missed opportunity for healing. Some items hold layers of memories that may take several rounds of decluttering before you can eventually let them go. A wedding ring following a divorce, for example, may take several rounds of processing before you decide to sell it.

That being said, I urge you to push yourself beyond what might be comfortable. That will most likely entail feeling emotions that come up for an item. If you weren't ready, the item wouldn't be up for consideration to begin with. Our soul is always propelling us forward. These items from the past are the keys to moving us into the future.

In the next chapter, we will explore another relationship with which we strongly identify—our job or career. Women usually identify more with personal relationships, while men form their identity around their work. This is a general categorization and is changing quickly in our society as women are becoming more career-oriented and men are seeking more balance through relationships. Balancing relationships and careers—who we are at home and in the world—is a fine line that both genders are now dealing with.

In general, we all form our identity around whom we're with and what we do. Both of these areas provide a mirror for us and provide a platform for our soul's expansion. When one or both of these areas are in flux, we can be at a loss about who we are. This can also be a time of rapid spiritual growth. We no longer form an identity around our title, whether it is *Mrs.* or *CEO*. Instead, we're forced to look underneath the labels and uncover the truth within us. You may realize it's time for a clutter intervention of work-related items in order to fully step into the work you really want to be doing.

I Am What I Did

Past Careers and Jobs

When meeting someone for the first time, it doesn't take long before the question "What do you do?" is posed. Our work, job, vocation, or career is a big part of our identity. It defines who we are in the world. What we have to offer. Why we are here. What we are good at. What our talents are. It can even represent one's worth in the world, not to mention livelihood or basic means for survival.

Throughout our life, we go through many jobs, if not careers. For some people, jobs or careers are like a crescendo of stepping stones leading to a climatic role before finally retiring. For others, a career path may look like a hodgepodge of choices ultimately creating a beautifully constructed patchwork quilt. In either case, one's career path is often laden with unknowns and trepidation about the next step. Our career not only defines our identity in the world, but it's also the means to our livelihood.

When we are uncertain about our career or purpose, our identity also feels uncertain. I remember when my last contract job as an attorney ended. I hadn't fully embraced my new role in the healing arts yet, nor was it supporting me to the extent that being an attorney had. This spun me into a serious identity crisis. I had just purchased a new home and signed a rental lease on a healing space. It wasn't so much my identity as an attorney I had lost. My identity as a smart and fiscally responsible professional was over.

When your job has been pulled out from under you, it can be a jolt that triggers basic survival fears. As if a blow to one's self-esteem isn't enough, it can knock you on your knees and send you into a spiral of fear and confusion. The emotional consequences are usually not even dealt with because of the logistical ramifications of finding a new source of income.

However, if given the luxury of time after a sudden career shift, it's important to take time off for soul clarification. It's an opportunity to discover your true desires and to learn if you need a course correction to feel in alignment with your desired purpose. For some, it takes being kicked out of their comfortable job to finally put them on the path of their true desires. Getting fired or laid off can be a blessing in disguise in hindsight even though it doesn't feel that way in the moment. Instead of initiating a walk across a bridge, the universe nudges us off a cliff.

With the economy changing so drastically and quickly, many people are voluntarily opting to undergo a career change. Technological advances have opened new pathways for jobs and careers that didn't exist five years ago or even a year ago. Meanwhile, companies based on older ways of doing business are falling away. A new economy is emerging based on mobility, technology, social media, alternative medicines, energy resources, and new ways of learning.

As a result of these swift changes, many people are completely changing careers. For some, it's out of a need to adapt to the new economy. For others, their desire for more creative or heart-centered work has become too loud to ignore. Regardless, any change in career comes with doubt and confusion as you go through an identity change. Some can feel a little crazy turning in their six-figure corporate job to mix essential oils for a home-based business only because their intuition guided them to do so.

What I hear most from clients is the desire to be their own boss, have more flexibility, be more creative, do something they feel passionate about that also helps the world, and to have a better work-life balance. This seems to be an overarching theme in the workplace too as employers are accommodating these demands by providing better workspaces and more flexibility with telecommuting and scheduling.

Even when one voluntarily makes a job or career change, it takes time to adjust to the change. If it's been a complete career change, it will take time to morph into this new identity and fully embody it with confidence. It may take years in fact to fully make the transition. However, the more you understand what you're reluctant to let go of, the more the process can be expedited.

Even with previous jobs or careers we didn't like, there was still comfort in knowing who we were in that job. It took me years to fully let go of my attorney identity, even after I was no longer practicing law. There's always more below the surface of what we're really getting out of an identity. In addition to my identity around being fiscally responsible and secure, I realized I was also hanging on to the acceptance I received from family and society. In reality, it was just my perception of what is valued based on family programming.

I gradually transitioned into a healing arts practice. I was wearing multiple hats throughout the day. In the mornings from eight to noon, I practiced law. In the afternoon, I tended to interior design projects, and then at night I taught yoga. I was clearly in transition. Each role felt authentic to me at the time, although I was not fully committing to any of them. My heart was definitely moving toward the healing arts, while the law still gave me a sense of grounding and security.

Our attachment to our past work identity
is memorialized through work clothing,
old manuals, and even past awards.

As I built my healing arts practice, I slowly let the legal work go. Although there were practical considerations of affording a career change, I was also shifting my identity from being a practical, responsible attorney to a woo-woo spiritual seeker and teacher. Other people may choose a more direct path. In either case, it takes time to adapt to a new identity. This is evident by the things we hold on to from past jobs and careers. Our attachment to our past work identity is memorialized through work clothing, old manuals, and even past awards. Let's take a closer look at these items and what they represent.

Career Clothing

Our clothing is a personal uniform we put on each morning as we go out into the world. Who will you be today? What persona will you take on? What identity will you try on? This is all represented in the clothing we wear. In times when we are going through identity shifts, or even just days we're extra moody, we may struggle with what to wear. This is why adolescents' wardrobes may vary greatly from one day to the next. Some days they are a chameleon and match what their friends are wearing, and other days they are more avant-garde in exploring different personas.

In some cultures, religions, or even niche societies, there's a standard of what to wear in order to be consistent with the group's overall identity. There is no room for individual expression. This may be the case for some corporate cultures with a strict dress code. Many professions have an official uniform, such as police officers, service specialists, and hospitality professionals. Professionalism is often marked by a cohesive and predictable standard of clothing.

Whether you had an official uniform, corporate-logo shirt, or a standard set of outfits you wore in a former profession, you immediately associate those clothes with that job or career. Letting go of those clothes is a strong statement of letting go of the related identity, whereas holding on to them means you haven't had full closure with that time of your life.

It took me years after practicing law before I finally let go of my last business suit. Even though I had no desire to practice law or even wear business clothes ever again, a pin-striped Banana Republic business suit still hung in my closet. My excuse was to keep it just in case I needed a business suit one day. The *just in case* excuse is covered in more detail in chapter 8. As you probably guessed, it's always a cover for something deeper. Even though I thought I had completely disidentified with being an attorney, the suit was evidence that there was at least 1 percent left to release. Once I finally let the business suit go, there was a sudden influx of new healing clients the following week.

Anytime you still have energy in the past, it will prevent you from completely moving all your energy into the present. Our belongings represent our energy and will give clues to what past job or career may still be lingering in the present. I had one client who was hanging on to work clothes from a corporate job she quit years ago. She couldn't understand why she was still keeping her business clothes, especially since her yoga clothes were her typical outfit as a stay-at-home mom and yoga enthusiast. Her excuse was *just in case* she needed them again one day, even though she admitted that they were out of style and she had no desire to wear them ever again.

After I prompted her with a few questions, she realized the clothes represented an old identity of being successful, independent, and productive. Not only did it allow her to get clear about her current choice to not work, but she was able to validate for herself that being a stay-at-home mom is the best decision for her right now. She was then able to let go of the clothes with ease and a sense of accomplishment. This was the case with my situation too. When I realized the attorney suit represented my past, I put a new stake in the ground, owning my new role and identity as a holistic practitioner.

Take a look in your closet and see if you're hanging on to clothes representing a past job or career. It could be an actual uniform you had to wear for a job or clothing you wore during that time of your life when you were in the past job or career. Think about what identity that job or career gave you and how you might still be relying on it for some sense of validation. Even if you've already made the career change and moved through the related emotions, you may need to simply acknowledge it. In doing so, this completes the past identity and allows you to fully move into the present.

This inquiry is also useful if you have not yet moved into the new job or career and are looking to do so. The case with our relationship with our work is the same as romantic relationships: it's important to release items from the past one to attract a new one. If you're getting hung up on what's next regarding your career, see what you can release from the past. This will clear stagnant energy and allow you to more clearly focus on what you truly want to do. Clear out old identities in order to create space for the new you to emerge.

Papers and Manuals

We live in the age of information. It's all around us. Knowing what to keep and what not to keep can feel like a daunting task.

Will I need this information later?

I don't want to waste this information.

What if I need it later and don't have it?

I may need to reference it later.

These are a few of the reasons we hold on to papers, manuals, workbooks, directories, or any other type of information from a previous job or career.

Investing in our own skills and talents is the most valuable commodity when it comes to our work in the world. Having particular knowledge or having access to certain information is part of what makes us valuable. It significantly contributes to our identity and bolsters our confidence in a field. It's no wonder we're afraid of tossing it out too quickly, particularly if it once made us money or led to our current level of success.

Unfortunately, though, information starts to stack up. Binders, workbooks, files, directories, and books can quickly take up important shelf space and lead to a cluttered office. When does valuable information turn to clutter and become a vestige of the past? In other words, when does information become stagnant and create a negative energy in one's life instead of positive energy?

There are several considerations for determining whether to keep information from the past. First, ask yourself why you think you should keep it and how realistic your reasoning is. If it's been several years since you've referred to the information, then there's probably another reason you're hanging on to it. Most likely, you're attached to the idea of holding on to the information more so than you are really in need of it. The ego will paperclip itself to anything and keep you stuck like sticky notes.

I had one client unsure about what to do with old training manuals from a healing arts modality she studied years ago. She admitted they were taking up valuable space in her office. But when it came time to clear them out, she was reluctant, just in case she might need them again. She had not referred to them in years. Whenever your first impulse is to clear something out and then you start to question yourself, there's usually more to the story than you might think. After asking her a few questions, she realized the manuals represented an older aspect of her work that was no longer applicable.

Hanging on to old information can be similar to using training wheels when you don't really need them anymore.

Hanging on to old information can be similar to using training wheels when you don't really need them anymore. It changes from being a crutch to impeding you from fully stepping into your power. Maybe you're the expert and should now be writing your own manual. Or perhaps it's worth your time to flip through the information and keep pages that could be helpful. Throw out the bulky, unneeded information so that it's not taking up so much space. I keep a file folder of tear-outs from larger manuals to save space.

I had another client who was holding on to years and years of medical journals she received bimonthly as a medical doctor. They were taking over her office, and yet she felt like she needed to keep them. After a few questions, it was clear that she felt guilty for not reading them. Her excuse was to keep them with the intention of reading them one day or at least refer to them just in case she needed to reference an article.

Neither of those situations had yet happened in all her years of collecting the journals. Instead, she was setting herself up for an insurmountable goal that she was failing at each and every time she looked at the journals. Meanwhile, the evidence of being "not good enough" as a doctor was literally stacking up around her. Holding on to the journals represented the identity of being a responsible doctor, but underlying that was the sabotaging thought of failing to be a responsible doctor. She admitted that she didn't really need to read the articles for her work, but it seemed like the responsible thing to do.

If you haven't used the information and still feel hesitant to get rid of it, ask yourself more questions. What are you really afraid of throwing away? Is there an image of yourself that you associate with the information? What identity are you afraid to throw away? Does the information keep you in the past or springboard you into the future? Are you keeping it out of fear or abundance?

> We take in new information upon first receiving it, when it feels new, fresh, and exciting. After that, it's old news.

In most cases, if you haven't referred to certain information for some time, you most likely won't. We take in new information upon first receiving it, when it feels new, fresh, and exciting. After that, it's old news. It served its purpose. In most cases, information is now readily available through online services. Most information that you legitimately might need just in case can be found online, at your fingertips, without cluttering up your office space.

Supplies

In addition to saving outdated information, holding on to old supplies is another tactic for holding on to past careers. For most jobs or careers, you need supplies, which could be anything from pencils to paint brushes to printer ink. Supplies that we're no longer using can trip us up in determining whether to keep or not because of their potential practical application. In tossing around the practicalities in our head, we bypass and underestimate the emotional considerations that are really underlying the decision-making process.

It took me years to finally part with my Prismacolor marker collection that I used for an architectural rendering side business. Not only did they provide me with a nice income during that time, but they were also quite valuable themselves. However, they were not valuable to anyone while they sat in my closet. A few years after I stopped doing renderings, I sold my marker collection on eBay to a design student. She was thrilled to have them. In hindsight, I was holding on to the markers not out of practicality but out of identity. I was still holding on to the identity of an interior designer. It really wasn't just the identity of an interior designer, but that of an *artistic* interior designer.

Being artistic was an identity that I was able to embrace in interior design school after not feeling creative most of my life. Being creative was my mom's identity, and I didn't think I could fill her shoes. Those markers were evidence that I was artistic, particularly since they contributed to me winning many design awards. Once I acknowledged that those artistic talents are a part of everything I do, I was able to let them go. I haven't missed the markers, and my only regret is that I didn't sell them sooner in order to step into a more integrated version of my creativity.

For creatives, supplies are the instruments with which they make art or gain inspiration. Unused supplies, on the other hand, will do the opposite and end up stagnating the creative process. I often see this situation with artist clients. They keep old art supplies or inspiration files even if they haven't touched them in years for fear of losing their inspiration. However, this couldn't be further from the truth. If it hasn't given you inspiration yet, then it probably won't. Inspiration happens in a flash, in peak moments of life, not in piles from yesteryear.

Inspiration happens in a flash,
in peak moments of life,
not in piles from yesteryear.

This is also the case with business professionals and outdated office supplies. Even though office supplies are more pragmatic in their application, their use is as important as paintbrushes are to an artist. Supplies become antiquated or inoperable and end up getting stashed away. They end up taking up valuable space in credenzas and on shelves, lending to cluttered surface areas.

The typical reason I hear from clients for keeping old supplies is *just in case* they might need them again. After I ask a few questions, they usually realize they don't need the item and easily toss it. In some cases, it's not so clear-cut because there is a former identity at stake. The supplies represent a former job or task that they are not ready to let go of.

If you have some old work supplies hanging around, think about your job, title, or the work with which the supplies are associated. Acknowledge how that time in your life contributed to your overall career and where you are now. Most likely, the supplies represent a limited aspect of a larger mosaic of your life purpose. In seeing the bigger picture, you can let go of the old supplies and step more fully into the expanded version of your current self.

Awards

It's easy to make excuses for keeping old supplies, clothing, papers, and manuals, and it's even easier to justify keeping old awards. After all, they are reminders of positive accolades, right? Yes, but not so fast. Awards are seemingly benign objects, but they can keep you stuck in the past more so than you might think. We tend to think of clutter as items that take us back to not-so-good times in our lives, but clutter can also be items that represent the good times too. Clutter is anything that keeps us anchored in the past, preventing us from moving forward. This even includes times when we were awarded or recognized for a particular achievement.

We tend to think of clutter as items that take us back to not-so-good times in our lives, but clutter can also be items that represent the good times too. Clutter is anything that keeps us anchored in the past, preventing us from moving forward.

Awards include plaques, trophies, photos, or any other tangible items that memorialize an honor. These awards might be displayed or stored in a filing cabinet or closet. In either case, it's possible they are keeping you stuck in the past. That being said, I'm certainly not suggesting you throw out all your awards. After all, they represent successes that should be acknowledged and celebrated. Awards can also be used to positively energize a space when they are in alignment with your current job or career. Whether an award constitutes clutter is a person-by-person and item-by-item determination.

A clutter intervention is called for if you feel stuck in your current work situation. Stuckness is the byproduct of lack of clarity, lack of clarity is a byproduct of stagnation, and stagnation is a byproduct of having one foot in the past. During transitional times, it's understandable to have one foot in the old world and one foot in the new world. However, if this goes on for too long, you will start to feel stuck. When this happens, it's usually out of fear of the unknown.

You may have a desire for something new and different, but there's also a fear of giving up the old comforts and even a track record of successes. At least in the old world you knew who you were and were even praised for it. Who knows who you'll be if you let that identity go? These subconscious conversations are the reason we hold on to awards even if they are outdated and no longer applicable to the work we are doing now or want to be doing.

Another consideration is if the award is pertinent to your current job or career. Are you holding on to winning *Best Salesman—1998* when you are now in a managerial position in a different line of work? Are you relying on your past laurels to prove to yourself or others that you are worthy of your current position? Do you need reminding of your worth? If the award or other professional acknowledgment, such as certificates and diplomas, is related to your current position, then display it proudly. However, reconsider if it relates to a profession or title completely unrelated to your present position.

Awards are confidence boosters. They may be beneficial to display, even if outdated, until you've established a new level of confidence in a new vocation. They can provide a nice reminder of your skills and talents. Be mindful, however, of when they outwear their usefulness and if they start to hold you back from gaining achievements in your new line of work. The positive times in life should never hold you back but always propel you forward. This is true not only in work situations but in all areas of your life.

CHAPTER 5

The Glory Days
Past Associations,
Accomplishments, and Stories

If your identity is not attached to your career, then perhaps it is with a particular association, accomplishment, or experience in your life. Identity can become frozen in time around past associations that were significant in some way, such as being a mother, captain of the football team, PTO president, or homecoming queen. Some people also identify with experiences, such as attending a certain school, living in a particular city, or their exotic travels. Memorabilia from these times provide evidence of these notable events in life.

These special times in our lives give us a sense of uniqueness, a sense of belonging, an establishment of reputation, a feeling that we are special. In other words, we like our identity around such associations. We are proud of ourselves for these times and want the acknowledgment to continue from ourselves and others. Although they may have been fleeting moments in the past, we hold on to them. Instead of integrating the experiences, they become hallmarks of one's identity.

These peak moments are flashes along our timeline and are dedicated to a certain time in our life. When enjoyed in balance, each success can build upon the previous one to create a pattern of successes that form a longer, more sustainable identity. However, if we get stuck on a previous success or association, it leaves no room for new experiences to come in. Our identity becomes a statue of the past.

Items memorializing these times, such as logo T-shirts, trophies, photos, mugs, a child's pacifier, a letterman jacket, plaques, or other memorabilia, are like time capsules. Positive memories certainly have their place, but many people view, consciously or unconsciously, these times as the best days of their life. If that is an unconscious belief, then it will in fact become true.

We have many more future identities to try on and experiences to have. It's only when we get stuck in the past that we fulfill our prophecy that the best times are behind us. Saving items in the name of memorabilia can be a cover excuse for keeping you stuck in that time. Good memories can clutter up our lives, just like the not-so-good memories. This prevents new experiences from coming in, and over time we will feel stuck in our life.

Similar to saving awards related to one's job or career as discussed in the previous chapter, holding on to items related to a past association or accomplishment can prevent forward motion if you're not careful. There's a fine balance between celebrating the good times in our life and moving forward into the future. What may seem like innocent memorabilia could be a subconscious trap keeping you stuck in the past.

The telltale sign that your energy is being consumed by the past is if you feel stuck in your life. Do you feel like you're in a rut or that life is passing you by? Do you look to the past as the best days of your life? Do you feel like you're just spinning your wheels in life like a hamster on a wheel? If any of these scenarios strike a cord with you, then it may be time for a clutter intervention of items that represent past experiences. Over time, stagnation can lead to depression, lethargy, confusion, and hopelessness.

What's really at the core of the issue is a lack of a new identity, or sense of self. The past identity is gone by virtue of the ticking clock, but there is confusion about what's next. One example is the empty-nester mom. The eighteen-year (or more) identity of being a mom with dependents is no longer prevalent in daily life.

Who am I if I'm not a mom?

Who am I without taking care of others?

What do I do now?

This can be an extremely confusing time. The longer you try to hang on to the old identity that has passed you by, the longer you will feel stuck and the deeper the confusion. This is true with any past identity.

The best approach in such situations is to take time to grieve what has passed. This is usually the step we try to skip over and quickly distract ourselves with busyness. Instead, acknowledge your sadness from the passing of whatever identity or experience is no longer a part of your life. (We will talk more about the grief process in chapter 6.)

Another common example I see with clients is the loss of identity as a result of moving to a new city. This is most common when the move is the result of an involuntary job transfer or that of a spouse. Suddenly, they are uprooted from a city or neighborhood they loved. They try to make the best of their situation but can't seem to get grounded in the new city or their new home. Clients often believe something is wrong with their home when it's really their resistance to the bigger picture.

Transitions take time, but at the root of the distress is that the former city and former life hasn't been grieved. When this happens, there is inherent resistance to the new situation that prevents a natural flow of life to take place. This could include being a vibrational match to a house with feng shui problems, and so their concerns are valid. But it's part of a bigger energetic pattern that they're undergoing in their transition. We usually think of the need to grieve in terms of people or animals, but it also applies to places or anything from our past.

The final outcome of grieving is acceptance of your current situation. Accept that the past has passed in order to iron out the energetic bumps. Once you arrive at this point, the new can start to come in much quicker. In the case with empty-nester moms, this may be a time of self-exploration of what now interests you. The new identity may take time to develop as you discover new aspects of yourself that were not logistically feasible or accessible to you during your primary role as a mother.

The stuff from the past that we hang on to is a sign of what past identities we're hanging on to, from the baby pacifiers to the tattered *New York, New York* sweatshirt. Everything on the outside is a mirror for what's on the inside. Using those items as a way to process the past is a great way to help move forward. The following sections explore some of the common identities we shift through and the related items we hold on to as a result.

Parenthood

It's a common struggle among parents to know how much of their kids' stuff they should keep. Be mindful that keeping things for when your children are grown can be a common excuse for holding on to the past yourself. This all-too-common excuse is discussed in more detail in chapter 8. It's easy to pass the baton to others when it's really your own emotions that need to be processed. Your child's toy from when they were five years old is more than the memory around that time. It also represents your identity as a mother. This is often why mothers hold on to items when it makes little sense to do so.

> Your child's toy from when they were five years old is more than the memory around that time. It also represents your identity as a mother.

I had one client who kept all her kids' pacifiers in a ziplock baggie as keepsakes. These were only a few of the hundreds, if not thousands, of toys and clothes she kept stored in several closets. There was not a chance she was going to forget about those precious years with her children. There was also little chance she was going to move forward into her new life anytime soon. She was holding firmly to her identity of being a mother, more specifically a mother of young children. A mother is always a mother, but at stake are those years when her day-to-day life revolved around her kids' activities.

Women who married and had children at a young age may have missed a chance to establish their own identity beyond being a wife and mother. Their life orbited around serving the needs of their family. When the kids move out of the house, they are at a loss for where to direct their energy. They are forced to figure out who they are while also grieving their role as mother.

During this transition, it's most likely too difficult to declutter kids' items. In fact, it's a time when holding on feels more in alignment than letting go. Over time, however, decluttering can be an opportunity to loosen your grip around the role and old identity. When the nudge comes to start paring down items, it's common to feel at a loss with what to do with kids' memorabilia.

Children's Memorabilia

As adult children chart their own path, they no longer live at home but still have personal items there. If space is limited, this can cause logistical issues for parents. While they want to oblige their kids, they also need space. For some parents, there is a comfort knowing their kids' stuff is still in the home even if square footage is an issue.

Many baby boomers are feeling a real desire to lighten their loads, including their kids' stuff. It's common for adult children to not want to deal with their possessions either due to lack of space or a more mobile lifestyle. As a result, parents feel stuck with a bunch of stuff and overwhelmed with what to do with it all. They feel guilty for getting rid of it but claustrophobic by keeping it.

Anytime you store items for someone else, it's an allowance of their energy in your space. It is a literal and energetic boundary that is being compromised. This line is easily blurred among family members, evidencing a common codependent relationship pattern. It's often challenging to know where love and dependence begin and end. Related or not, it's important to be conscious of whose energy you are allowing in your space. It's a mirror of the energetic relationship between you and that person.

We usually don't think twice about storing things for children or other relatives, unless it starts impinging upon our physical boundary. Here are some tips for dealing with all the stuff:

- If your children are grown, have them go through their memorabilia to see what they want to keep. If they keep putting the task off, then give them a time limit. *You have until this time next year to go through this, and after that it's going to charity.* Remind them as their deadline gets closer. You have to stick with the boundary you set. Your kids are most likely avoiding their own cathartic process that comes with decluttering. You're not the only one who wants to avoid it. Give them the right of first refusal and have them take ownership of what they want to keep.

After all, it's their crayoned artwork, graduation cap, and pictures from high school.

- As long as you continue to offer to store stuff for your kids, they will want to keep most things. Adult children find comfort in keeping items at their childhood home and will often be reluctant to go through them. If your children are not adults yet, then they don't have adequate hindsight to know what they will want to keep. In this case, gather the memorabilia and store it in organized containers until they are old enough to go through it.

- After your children have taken what they want, the rest is yours. This may vary from rooms full of stuff to a file folder. Everyone is different in the amount they accumulate and therefore with the amount they want to keep or get rid of.

- Select a container size for what you want to keep. Your ideal size may be a file folder, a storage bin, a closet, or even a room. Decide what is best for you. If you select a large bin, add your favorite items until the bin is full. And that's it. Clear out the remaining items.

- Some people suggest taking photos of memorabilia and then disposing of the items. If this appeals to you, then this could certainly lighten your load. With a picture you don't get the sensory experiences of touch and smell that you get with the actual item, but it may be better than forgetting the memory altogether and allow you to let go of the actual item.

Being a parent is a vital part of one's identity. Paring down items that represent the heart of those memories can be challenging. With or without the items, your relationship with your child or children will continue as they grow into adulthood. Make room for new memories. Chapters are always closing with new ones opening. The same is true when the time comes to move to a new city. A new story is beckoning, but are you allowing it to be told?

Association with Cities

The ego will form an identity around anything. It craves a sense of belonging while also needing to feel special. This has been key to our survival for eons. If you were cast out from the tribe, you were left to fend for yourself, which meant death sooner rather than later. Even now that survival is not so much the issue, feeling a sense of belonging where you live is important to having a sense of peace, harmony, and grounding. For some, a strong sense of identity is formed around a neighborhood or city. Most people don't realize how much they associate with where they live until it comes time to move from that area.

When I moved from Nashville to Los Angeles, it took close to three years to fully transition into feeling at home. Luckily, I had already started to let go of my identity around Nashville, in addition to the trendy neighborhood I had lived in for over ten years prior to the move. Even though it was a voluntary move, it was still difficult and took time for me to adjust. Even good change is difficult.

As social beings, it's important to feel a sense of belonging within a community. However, when and if the time comes to move, a strong identification with the previous area can become a stumbling block. There can be such a strong hold on the former location that it makes it difficult to integrate into the new area. This is of course understandable, as all transitions take time. Our sense of belonging in the world is shaken because our identity no longer has a secure attachment to a location. Just like with past careers or relationships, there can be a gap in which you feel a loss of who you are as it relates to a particular sense of self.

Our identification with locations is often represented through our stuff, such as bumper stickers, T-shirts, memorabilia from local events, or event posters. I've worked with clients who have difficulty settling into their new home and life following a move due to their sense of identity around their former location. This can also create an energetic block for selling a home in their former location after already having moved. Their heartstrings are still with the former community. As a result, they have an energetic hold on the home, making it difficult for a new buyer to come in.

If you find that you are having
difficulty emerging in a new community,
consider what you haven't let go from
the former location.

If you find that you are having difficulty emerging in a new community, consider what you haven't let go from the former location. Just like any loss, there is a need to grieve the past so as to move into the new. Acknowledging the loss and what you miss, as opposed to forcing a smile on your face and forging through your day, can expedite the process. Use items representing the former location to process the emotions. Oftentimes, people will decorate their home with items from a city to which they have allegiance. If you are having difficulty moving on, consider whether this is in your best interest or not.

Even if you have a desire to return one day to the former location, it's important to embrace where you currently are. There's always a reason why we're where we are. Or maybe you experienced the "geographical cure," a common predicament in which we think a different city will solve our problems. Although transitions take time, be conscious of whether you are identifying more with the past or the present. Where your attention goes, energy flows.

High School or College Personas

High school or college can be some of the best years of life or some of the worst. With a microscope on social inclusion, you can sink or swim depending on where you are within the social ranks. I was never sure of my identity as I floated around from group to group. I fit in everywhere and nowhere. For people who clearly knew their identity during these times, it most likely served them well by helping them understand where they fit in school and later in the world.

The ego loves recognition of any kind
and will hang on to it however it can,
especially if it worked out positively
at a young age.

The ego loves recognition of any kind and will hang on to it however it can, especially if it worked out positively at a young age. This can make change more difficult and is one reason child actors struggle later in adulthood. Early social titles, such as *star quarterback*, *homecoming queen*, or *most talented* are great acknowledgments that help shape one's self-esteem in a positive way. That can also make it difficult to move on when that era has passed and why letting go of the letterman jacket, the sorority swag, or other memorabilia from those times is otherwise unexplainably difficult.

A spouse or friend may question your judgment for hanging on to these items that seem to have no intrinsic value. What they don't realize is that it's like suggesting you cut off your left arm. At the root of that item is a core identity that the person is hanging on to from the past and that significantly shaped who they are. The identity could also simply be their youthful self.

It's common to keep items from these times for purposes of nostalgia. However, you should question whether the nostalgia is positively or negatively contributing to your life. If the memories are positive, they may provide a sense of self that builds confidence and is enjoyable to reminisce over. However, if those times seem more like the glory days when life was as good as it gets, then it's time to ask yourself if the past is keeping you from moving forward.

Items from our glory days remind us of our youthfulness, popularity, sense of adventure, independence, fun party days, or simply feeling carefree with no responsibilities. By keeping these reminders around, we live vicariously through them as if they are still relevant in some way. If you struggle with too much stuff from these times of your life, then consider ways to integrate these feelings into your current life.

The nostalgic items may give you clues as to what you would like more of in your current life. Instead of getting stuck in the past, bring new, fun experiences into your current life. In the next section, you'll see how we can also get stuck in our old stories, preventing new ones from coming in. Never underestimate your power in creating new memories.

Our Stories and Experiences

Past identities stem not only from our early years but also from more recent events in adulthood. These include unique experiences, like trekking Mt. Kilimanjaro or a personal story of surviving cancer. These are significant events and experiences that shape who we are. Our story may involve triumphantly facing the odds and coming out on the other side alive. It may be our hero's journey story with which we help inspire others.

The story I told for years was my journey of transitioning from an attorney to a healing arts practitioner. It's a good story and one that I continue to tell to inspire others, but I started to get tired of hearing it. I was ready for a new one. Your unique experiences and stories will always be a part of you. No one can take that away from you. But it's easy to get stuck in your story. In doing so, it can prevent you from moving forward to create new ones.

If your life has become consumed by your story, there will be physical evidence of it in your home. And it's most likely displayed for people to see. The more open you are about telling people your story, the more prominently displayed it is. For example, it may be depicted in photos hanging in the living room. However, if it's an inner story that you keep to yourself, then it may be hidden away from public viewing.

Is your story still serving you? If not, then consider decluttering items related to your story. This might include photos, print and digital, of certain events. I recently came across tons of pictures from my trip to Europe and Russia, which I took when I was in high school. The album was huge and taking up valuable space. When I flipped through it, I realized that most of the pictures meant nothing to me.

I realized I had felt a need to keep the memories alive because it was such an incredibly life-changing experience. But those memories were integrated and shaped me years ago. The photos will never depict the experience of that trip. More importantly, space needed to be cleared for more amazing travel experiences in my life. I kept the historical photos of Russia from the 1980s and trashed the big binder album to lighten my load. Now it's time to create new travel experiences.

Our story is an important narrative that gives meaning to our life. Stories help us make sense of our life in hindsight. But are you re-creating the same life over and over? If so and you desire something different, then stop telling your old story and live to create a new one. Your life is a prism of experiences, and, depending on what angle you look at it, you can tell a different story.

If your story carries a theme of victimhood or martyrdom, then it may be time to reshape it to reflect empowerment. Or maybe it's time for a new story altogether. By changing your view of the past, you shape your future. Making peace with the past is essential to creating the life you want. The next chapter will help you address any unhealed wounds, release unresolved grief, move past the old stories, and finally make peace with your stuff.

CHAPTER 6

What Could Have Been

Unhealed Wounds and Unresolved Grief

In the preceding chapters, you've seen how easy it is to hang on to the past—the good times and the bad. You most likely recognized your tendencies and how the past has shown up in the stuff you hold on to. Not releasing the past can be a stumbling block to fully moving forward into the life you want to be living. When negative emotions stew for too long, the problem is further compounded. If left unattended, unpleasant emotions turn toxic and bitterness sets in. Our belongings become permanent fixtures for disguising the underlying pain.

If you've read up to this point and still find it difficult to get rid of certain items, then this may be the chapter you've been waiting for. When we hold on to things that are no longer serving us, there are usually unhealed wounds or unresolved grief associated with it. It's easy to avoid dealing with the past until it becomes so much a part of our present that we can no longer ignore it. This could come in the form of physical discomfort, destructive relationship patterns, or severe anxiety or depression.

It's best to address the past before it causes us more pain in the future. These past wounds usually get our attention through triggers. Triggers are events or situations in the present that elicit an overreaction because they mimic a wound from our past. These triggers alert us to an unhealed wound. Therapeutic and healing methods, such as eye movement desensitization and reprocessing, hypnotherapy, or inner child work can be invaluable for processing these unhealed wounds.

It's easy to brush triggers off
as something someone else is causing,
but it's really a reaction to a
deep wound within ourselves.

It's easy to brush triggers off as something someone else is causing, but it's really a reaction to a deep wound within ourselves. While someone may be unfairly provoking us or causing us pain, we continue to attract these situations to us until the pain is finally addressed and processed. Our soul is always moving toward healing and wholeness and will continue to attract situations until the underlying issue is finally in our rearview mirror. We energetically match up to situations because they are active in our energy field. What you might think of as karma at play bringing people and situations to you is simply energy—like energy attracting like energy.

Throughout life, we inevitably suffer loss and experience disappointments. In *The Five Things We Cannot Change*, psychotherapist David Richo presents five unavoidable truths that we all face throughout life:

1. Everything changes and ends.
2. Things do not always go according to plan.

3. Life is not always fair.

4. Pain is part of life.

5. People are not loving and loyal all the time.

None of us are immune to these truths. And yet it's easy to slip into victimhood to life's circumstances when bad things happen. If the pattern continues, our emotions will eventually turn to regret and resentment.

Richo points out that inherent within each of these seemingly negative events are also gifts. For example, with all endings come beginnings that keep life fresh and new. When things don't go according to plan, it's usually because there is a grander plan in place that we can't see. When we don't cling tightly to a plan, we allow synchronicities into our life and allow space for the Divine to show off its magic. The cliché "rejection is protection" is a perfect example. Oftentimes we think we want something, and when we don't get it, we feel like the universe is playing us for a fool. We later realize that there was something even better awaiting us.

The third principle, life is not always fair, can feel like a harsh reminder of the injustices in our life. But with this we cultivate compassion for others who have also suffered losses. This gives us a greater capacity to love and puts us on an equal playing field with humanity. This leads to the fourth principle, that pain is a part of life. Unfortunately, pain and suffering are still a major part of life here on earth. It has been the avenue through which most of us make our greatest transformations. It's also been the primary path for enlightenment masters, such as Buddha and Jesus.

The fifth unavoidable truth, according to Richo, is that people are not loving or loyal all the time. This is often what triggers us the most because our greatest healing takes place in our relationships. Everyone is walking around wearing their own wounds on their sleeves. While we may take it personally when someone hurts us, this is part of the human experience. When we begin to trust and rely on ourselves, we are not at the mercy of others making us happy. This state of being will also attract more trustworthy people into your life.

We usually think of grief as something
that only pertains to a physical death,
but it equally applies to the ending
of relationships, places, and situations
in our life.

When any of these unavoidable givens shows up in our life, we are faced with accepting it. In other words, we must employ the grief process with people and situations that don't go the way we had wished. We usually think of grief as something that only pertains to a physical death, but it equally applies to the ending of relationships, places, and situations in our life. Endings are part of the human experience, but we try to skip over them. Most of us are open to new things, but not at the expense of letting go of the old. New beginnings are only possible after something else is complete.

People change out of pain or pleasure, and in most cases it's pain. Feeling and acknowledging the pain is crucial to moving through it. It is in our distraction techniques where we typically get stuck. This is where clutter comes in. Clutter is an avoidance tactic used to distract us from dealing with painful emotions from the past. Clutter keeps us in the shallow end of the pool to avoid the deep end, and yet we end up drowning in all the stuff.

Clutter keeps us in the shallow end of
the pool to avoid the deep end, and yet
we end up drowning in all the stuff.

With the fast pace of our current culture, our distraction tactics have only gotten more sophisticated. Even some aspects of spirituality can be used as distraction. In some ways, we're still looking for a quick fix or a magic pill. We've simply traded the prescription pill for the spiritual pill to avoid pain. I grew up in my dad's pharmacy, watching customer after customer pick up their prescription pills. Seeing this was a driving force behind me entering the healing arts where preventative medicine and other healing techniques are utilized.

I'm happy to see more and more people turning to alternative approaches and realizing the prescription pill isn't a cure after all. That being said, as a self-help practitioner and teacher myself, I see many people looking to the next energy session, angel card reading, self-help program, astrology transit, or spiritual teacher to instantly change their life. It's easy to get hooked into believing that the next one or the next one or the next one will be *the one* that turns everything around.

The only way to truly find peace and joy is by facing our demons, our shadows—in other words, our emotions—that we have buried for decades if not lifetimes. This is not an overnight process and is much harder to sell. It's a lifelong process of unraveling the layers of the human experience. As Carl Jung said in *Psychology and Alchemy*, "People will do anything, no matter how absurd, in order to avoid facing their own soul." [4] We will do just about anything to avoid the emotional body.

Alternative approaches have provided us more awareness and empowerment. This is a victory for sure. The problem, however, is that when painful emotions start to rear their head, we're actually able to push them back down with an affirmation, conscious thoughts, or even a meditation. This is far better than a synthetic pill that chemically

4. Carl Jung, *Psychology and Alchemy*, vol. 12, *The Collected Works of C. G. Jung* (Princeton, NJ: Princeton University Press, 1968), 99.

suppresses our emotions into dangerous side effects, but we are still skirting the underlying pain that is really driving the bus.

If you suppress one emotion, you suppress all emotions to the same extent. This is why true joy is elusive for most of us. We are still avoiding the only thing that will bring us true joy: going through the dark to find the light. Some of the best techniques for reaching the emotional body are body-centered modalities, which is why yoga has been a gateway for so many people in the healing arts. Inner child work also reaches those buried emotions because it is in childhood where all our pain begins.

Self-help techniques are at their best when they help us integrate the subconscious and conscious or, in other words, bring our shadows into the light. Until and unless we are ready to face the emotional body, we will still be reaching for that magic pill. Like a child, what our emotions really want is to be acknowledged, validated, heard, and felt, not covered up, bargained with, shamed, or bought off.

Like a child, what our emotions really
want is to be acknowledged, validated,
heard, and felt, not covered up,
bargained with, shamed, or bought off.

Clutter is like the prescription pill. It's used to cover up the pain. This is why most people avoid decluttering. A certain item triggers the emotional body and confusion sets in. You're suddenly overwhelmed or stopped in your tracks. The mind tries to make sense of the item—to keep or not to keep—but it becomes a mental ping-pong game full of the common cover excuses discussed in chapter 8. Instead, your soul is begging you to process it on the emotional level. When you approach decluttering through the lens of a healing method, you create the opportunity for real transformation, free of charge and prescription.

Sometimes we initiate endings and sometimes they are imposed upon us. The most common example is initiating the end of a relationship as opposed to the other person ending the relationship. In either case, there is an ending or loss that must be grieved or let go of in some way. Even with endings that we are happy about there is still a change afoot that's not necessarily easy.

With undesired endings, such as the end of a relationship, a job loss, or a death, our core belief about what our life is supposed to look like is challenged. We are grieving our belief system as much as the actual loss. For example, a mother grieves her future upon finding out her child is gay. *This isn't how I thought life was supposed to go.* A divorce can shake someone's beliefs about marriage. *I believed I would be with my spouse until death do us part.* Or a parent dies unexpectedly. *I assumed I would spend Christmas with my entire family.*

Times of grief are exceptionally difficult and call into question all our belief systems. Grief is nature's way of helping us deal with the natural process of loss and letting go. It's a letting go of the good times and the bad. It's proof that we loved and loved hard. I remember when I was seeing an EMDR therapist for processing early childhood wounds. I asked, "Now what about the good memories I have from my past relationship? How can I forget about those?"

She said, "Honey, that's called grief. It's nature's way of healing the past." I wanted a magic pill, but couldn't find one and had to face the grief process straight in the face.

The Process of Letting Go (Grief)

The grief process was first introduced by Elisabeth Kübler-Ross over thirty years ago in her book, *On Death and Dying,* and was more recently brought to mainstream psychology in *On Grief and Grieving,* cowritten with David Kessler. In these books Kübler-Ross describes the five stages of grief: denial, anger, bargaining, depression, and acceptance. Whether you are dealing with the physical death or emotional loss of a loved one, the grief process is equally applicable. In some cases, a breakup or divorce is as much of a loss, if not more, than a physical death. In either case, the person or life situation is no longer in your life. There is an ending and a loss. Life is forever changed but followed by a new beginning. The inevitable cycle of death and rebirth that we all experience is the cornerstone of Taoism and the basis of the five element theory used in feng shui.

In my book *Decorating with the Five Elements of Feng Shui*, the five element theory is explained in detail as it applies to your life and working with spaces. The five elements consist of Wood, Fire, Earth, Metal, and Water. These elements create the cycle of change. In essence, it's the cycle of birth, death, and rebirth. Everything in nature, including ourselves, goes through these cycles on a micro and macro level. On the macro level, life follows the five element cycle with birth and childhood as the Wood phase and ending later in our life in the Water phase. On the micro level, you can see the cycle play out in each day when you wake up to when you go to bed. The best example of the five element cycle is the seasons and how nature responds accordingly.

We all experience our own personal seasons of change. In times of grief, we are in the Metal and Water phases, whereas when things are going great in your life, you are in the Fire phase. When you start a new job or relationship, you are in the Wood phase. When life feels stabilized and grounded, you are experiencing the Earth phase. These phases ebb and flow throughout our life. The more you can flow with these phases, the more in alignment with your natural flow you will feel. This is the meaning of going with the flow. This is the *Way*, or *Tao*, and the core principle of Taoism.

What tends to happen, however, is we fight the flow. We try to go upstream or against the grain. This is resistance. This is feeling stuck.

And this is what happens when we try to skip over one of the phases, which is usually the Metal or Water phase, also known as grief or letting go of certain situations. Of course, it's also possible to dwell or get lost in this phase for too long or get too comfortable in the Earth phase and avoid the more outgoing (yang) phases of Wood and Fire.

We tend to gravitate to one or two of the phases and avoid other phases depending on our personality. Yang people tend to feel more comfortable in Wood and Fire, whereas yin people are more comfortable in Metal and Water phases. But each phase is a natural and necessary part of our life because change is a natural part of our life. Change is essential to expansion, and expansion is essential to our evolution. Only through endings can we have new beginnings.

The process of grief is an internal metamorphosis or rebirth within ourselves, similar to the hero's journey. It is nature's way of working through change and is essential to the human experience. To grieve is to be human and something most of us attempt to avoid in our fast-paced society, where distractions are more enticing than crying. But it is the window through which joy can truly be found.

Interestingly, Kübler-Ross's five stages of grief follow the natural cycles of nature that mirror the five elements in Taoism. The five stages of grief describe the more challenging aspects of each phase of the five elements. In the following sections, each grief stage is described in more detail. According to Kübler-Ross, it's common to vacillate among all the stages as opposed to experiencing them in a linear fashion. It's also common to spend more time in one of the stages than the others. For example, someone could spend their entire life in the anger phase. Obviously, this is not ideal. Others may spend years and years bargaining in a relationship until they finally accept it's over. Understanding these phases and using them as a guide can be helpful to understanding yourself, not to mention normalizing your own process.

Denial

The first stage of grief is denial. Denial can show up in a number of ways, depending on if it's a physical loss or emotional loss. When my mom passed away, I was not in denial that she actually died. I knew she died. But I was in disbelief.

How could this be?

How did this happen?

I can't believe she's gone.

For emotional losses, denial can show up in the form of disillusion. The denial stage can be a more literal denial of the reality of the situation.

I know he'll be back.

The relationship isn't over.

There's no way she just left.

He'll wake up and realize he made a mistake.

Denial can show up with any loss, from losing your job to losing your keys. The purpose of this phase is to help our mind manage the feelings—the trueness of the situation—so that we are not overwhelmed. It is for survival. As Kübler-Ross states, "It's nature's way of letting in only as much as we can handle."[5]

Anger

The next stage of grief is the anger phase. When you move into this phase, it means you're ready to feel emotion—not the root emotion quite yet, but at least some emotion. Anger is a cover emotion for the real pain, but it's the way out of the numbness experienced in the

---

5. Elisabeth Kübler-Ross and David Kessler, *On Grief and Grieving: Finding the Meaning of Grief Through the Five Stages of Loss* (New York: Scribner, 2005), 10.

denial stage. Kübler-Ross states that anger gives a "temporary structure to the nothingness of loss."[6]

The more you are able and willing to feel the anger, the quicker you will move through it. This is an essential part of the grief process, and people who've been taught that expressing anger is bad will often skip over it. When anger is not felt, it becomes suppressed and turns into bitterness. Bitterness is anger turned in on itself, and it comes out in passive-aggressive ways. When true anger is experienced, it will not last long. Paradoxically, the only way to get stuck in the anger phase is by not going into the anger.

It's preferable to find healthy outlets, although what's healthy is not always obvious after experiencing a huge loss. I remember my dad, who's normally a nice, considerate person, spewing out rude comments left and right to anyone and everyone during his grief process. Having a physical outlet for anger, which could be physical exercise, punching a pillow, or screaming and yelling in private, is advised.

The most important takeaway is that feeling anger is normal. Like the upcoming stage of depression, the anger phase isn't always appreciated, welcomed, or understood by those around you. But it's nonetheless important to experience. Kübler-Ross beautifully articulates the benefits of the anger stage: "Anger confirms that you can feel, that you did love, and that you have lost."[7]

Bargaining

When our emotions need a break, we go into the bargaining phase. The mental mind takes over to distract from the emotional pain. In the case of physical death, it's easy to start asking "if only" or "what if?" Our mind explores all the myriad ways we could have prevented the situation. In terms of emotional loss, bargaining can be similar to denial in that we bargain with ways to get the person back.

---

6. Ibid., 15.

7. Ibid., 16.

It wasn't that bad.

If I just change, it will be better.

If I go to therapy, he'll see that I've changed.

According to Kübler-Ross, "Guilt is often bargaining's companion."[8] It's easier to blame ourselves than feel the loss. With a physical death, bargaining usually pertains to what we could have done in the past to prevent the death. With nonphysical death, it relates to what we can do in the future to avoid the loss.

Maybe I can get my job back.

What if I agree to work longer hours?

I will cook dinner for him every night from now on.

The basis of our bargaining is the hope that through becoming a better person in some way, the loss can be reversed. Even if you are the one who instigated the ending of a relationship, the grief process equally applies and bargaining is still experienced.

If I'm nicer, things will be better.

What if I'm just more patient?

Him coming home drunk once a month isn't so bad.

In some relationships, both parties could stay in the bargaining phase for years, if not the entire marriage, before accepting that the relationship is dead and most likely has been for some time. Because the bargaining stage is a reprieve from feeling the emotional body, it can be a tempting place to hang out to avoid and numb the underlying pain of loss. This stage is similar to refusing the call in the stages of the hero's journey in that one is avoiding the next potentially painful step, which, in the case of the grief process, is depression.

---

8. Ibid., 17.

Depression

Depression is considered the last phase of the grief process before there is finally acceptance of the loss. This stage is usually what most people are trying to avoid because it feels like a dark pit from which you may never crawl out. The reality of the loss is no longer avoidable. You feel the pain. There's nothing left to bargain. And it feels like there's no point in living.

This stage can be confused for clinical depression. According to Kübler-Ross, "It's important to understand that this depression is not a sign of mental illness. It is the appropriate response to a great loss." [9] It is deep sadness. In our culture of the next shiny toy of distractions, we attempt to avoid sadness. If we're unable to distract enough, then we explain it away as a mental disorder. But when part of one's grief process, it is normal and necessary. Kübler-Ross explains that if you allow yourself to experience depression, "it will leave as soon as it has served its purpose in your loss." [10]

This stage is similar to the other emotion-filled stage of anger in that feeling the emotion and letting it wash through will allow it to process and then be on its way. Emotions are like ocean waves. Flow with them and they will pass. Resist them and you will get knocked down and caught in the undertow.

In my experiences with grief, I've learned the difference between what I call *good grief* and *bad grief*. Good grief feels like clean tears. When my mom passed away, I was also getting over a relationship. The difference in the tears became obvious to me. Good grief tears related to my mom's death felt clean, like ocean waves moving through me. Sometimes they were gentle waves and other times tsunami waves. They come over you in the most unpredictable times. In the moment, it feels overwhelming and then in minutes it's over. You feel renewed immediately following.

---

9. Ibid., 23.
10. Ibid., 22.

Bad grief, on the other hand, feels like dirty tears. These tears come with feelings of victimhood, rejection, and abandonment. They're ugly and seem unending. And yet they are as necessary as the good grief tears. The best approach is to accept the feelings you are feeling. Acknowledge them. Be with them, like a mother would be for a child. The bad grief will then transform into good grief.

Acceptance

The final stage of the grief process is acceptance. Acceptance doesn't mean you are okay with what happened, but that you accept that it has happened and have integrated it into a new sense of normalcy. You may not be pleased with the new situation, but there is relief. The grief is over and you can start anew.

In terms of a physical death, even though you may never be okay with the fact the person has died, you have accepted it and have a new sense or understanding of life without that person being in it. The same is true with the ending of a relationship. Even though you may not have wanted the ending, you accept it. In time, you may even have a bigger understanding of the role that person played in your life or see the silver lining of the situation. While this facilitates the ability to move on, acceptance can come with or without a broader perspective.

How fast or slow we move through these phases will depend on the severity of the loss. For example, if you get fired from a job that you didn't really like anyway, you might go through the stages in minutes. Your grief cycle may simply consist of calling up a friend and externally processing the following:

I can't believe this—I got fired (denial)! It was that asshole manager that was out to get me (anger). I wonder if I should talk to his boss and tell him the truth (bargaining). I really don't want to have to look for another job (depression). Oh, well. I'll miss my coworkers, but I'm sure I can find something better (acceptance).

You can see how grief shows up even in relatively minor events that we move through quickly. Major losses, on the other hand, can take years to process. If the grief process is avoided altogether, however, acceptance remains elusive. This can be the underlying root of clutter issues as the past piles up without proper grieving. In the case of departed loved ones, it can be helpful and even crucial to reach the acceptance phase of grief by sorting through the belongings related to that person.

Items of Departed Loved Ones

One of the most identity-shifting times in our lives is when a loved one passes. In addition to the grief and loss of a parent, spouse, child, friend, or lover, we also have to come to grips with who we are without them. *What will life be like now? How will I go on without this person? Who am I now that they are gone? Will I survive this loss?* In the literal death of that person's identity, we lose our own. We are forever changed by virtue of no longer relating to this person on the physical plane.

The only thing left of this person is their belongings. It's bittersweet. And handling the remnants of their energy is extremely challenging. However, if done consciously, it can assist the grief process. According to Kübler-Ross in *On Grief and Grieving*, "The ritual of dealing with a loved one's clothes and belongings facilitates the grieving process, partly by helping us accept the reality of the loss." [11] The grief process can't be rushed. It takes time and a huge dose of compassion for oneself.

Where one is in the process of dealing with the physical items is a reflection of where one is with the grieving process of that person. For example, if one is refusing to deal with the possessions of the deceased one, then they are experiencing the denial phase of grief. Once one gets the energy to address the physical items, the logistics

---

11. Kübler-Ross and Kessler, *On Grief and Grieving*, 136.

can feel conflicting and confusing. Mental clarity takes a backseat when emotions are activated, making everyday tasks seem challenging. This includes figuring out what to do with all the stuff.

Deciding What to Do with Items

The task of going through a loved one's belongings can be overwhelming. Kübler-Ross recommends starting this process only when you feel strong enough. Have friends or other family members help as much as possible. Just as you can't rush the grief process, you can't rush dealing with the possessions either. In fact, it's one and the same process. Don't feel pressured or rushed. If logistics are an issue, then store the items until you've had adequate time to sift, sort, and process the items and the emotions. When the acceptance stage of grief is reached, you will be ready to release the unwanted items.

What to do with the unwanted items, such as clothing, furnishings, and other personal items, will vary depending on the quantity. Once immediate family members have taken what they want, reach out to other friends and family members to see if they want any of the items before donating or selling to unrelated third parties. In cases where there is a large amount of stuff, an estate sale or auction may be needed.

Consider donating the proceeds or a portion of the proceeds to a cause in memory of the loved one. This will alleviate any concern with whether the items were let go appropriately. If items must be removed from their location immediately following the death, consider storing them temporarily. This will give family members time to make a clearer decision about what items to keep.

Inherited Items and Revisiting Items Later

For items of loved ones that you've kept, it's okay if your feelings about that decision change later. This is the case with items you inherited or voluntarily kept. Our relationship with our departed loved one is an evolving relationship, just as when the person was alive. Expanded perspective and awareness continues over time. Our desire to hold on to certain items may grow stronger or weaker with time. Don't feel obligated to keep items if you don't want them. That being said, if your reaction to get rid of certain items is part of the anger phase of grief, keep in mind your feelings will most likely change as you move into acceptance.

Our relationship with our departed
loved one is an evolving relationship,
just as when the person was alive.
Expanded perspective and awareness
continues over time.

If you're holding on to something out of obligation, then there's most likely an aspect of guilt involved. Items from loved ones should bring warm, loving memories, not guilt, shame, regret, or resentment. Are you holding on to an item out of pressure from other family members? Or is it your own sense of obligation? Think about if there is something unresolved between you and the person who has passed. The item could represent unresolved emotions that you are holding on to. Relationships can still be healed once someone has passed. Their spirit is available to make amends, and in fact with their expanded state, peace can be easily achieved.

Inheriting Your Own Items

When a parent or someone close to us passes, we might end up with our own items that we have to deal with. For example, if your parent was the keeper of your baby book, brass booties, and childhood photos, that's all yours now. You're the one that now has to decide to keep or not to keep these items from your past. The past is present for your review.

When we are suddenly faced with the past through our stuff, it's a time for reviewing our early years on a deeper level. Although you don't have to sort through it immediately, avoid packing it in a box, stuffing it in the attic, and forgetting all about it. The timing of items coming back to us is never random. It means the time is ripe for healing and integrating the past. Most importantly, don't store the items away just to pass the burden to others to sift and sort through once your time comes.

Think of these items as your golden ticket to more self-love. Once you realize you are now the keeper of your memories, you can be much more discerning and perhaps even more admiring of yourself. No one loves you more than yourself, and now you have the evidence to prove it. It's the perfect opportunity to release any negative emotions from the past that could otherwise become toxic emotions in the form of regret, resentment, and remorse.

Regret, Resentment, and Remorse

Not fully grieving losses or processing darker times can fester into regret, resentment, or remorse. In addition to leaving you stuck in the past, unresolved emotions can eventually find outward manifestation through the body in the form of disease, according to most alternative medicines and healing modalities, and in the home in the form of clutter.

Regret, resentment, and remorse are the most toxic emotions to harbor. What may seem like a typical storing of anger, either toward someone else or yourself, will become regret, resentment, or remorse if held over time. The same is true if we bury the anger or stay in denial that we were hurt at all. This can relate to people or situations from our past ranging from early childhood to more recent adulthood.

According to most alternative medicine approaches, including acupuncture, energy healing, and other mind-body modalities, holding in these emotions is detrimental to our physical health. In generations before psychotherapy was as widely used, the general approach was to just forget about and move on from traumatic events from our past. Now with the emergence of mind-body approaches to health, it's becoming more understood and accepted that our physical health is affected by our emotional and mental bodies. Stuck emotions in our body can eventually manifest in the physical body.

In my book *Mind, Body, Home*, I take the mind-body premise a step further and attribute symptoms in the home, such as a clogged toilet or a blown fuse, to imbalances in the mind and body. This is true for clutter too. If we're emotionally holding on to the past, then there will be items in the home memorializing it somewhere, either openly displayed or hidden away.

If you have a high volume of clutter, it's likely a subconscious distraction tactic to cover up regret, resentment, or remorse. The clutter contributes to keeping these heavy, dense emotions anchored in and covered up. The negative energy is simply projected back onto yourself and is in essence a form of self-betrayal. This is a toxic pattern that can eventually lead to physical disease.

When regret, resentment, or remorse is at the bottom of the pile and is really the core issue, the key is to pry one finger off at a time and move slowly into a place of freedom and allowance. It may be helpful to work with a therapist or healer to address emotions as they rise up in tandem with decluttering. As Zen master Thich Nhat Hanh said, "People have a hard time letting go of their suffering. Out of a fear of the unknown, they prefer suffering that is familiar." [12]

When these emotions are the root source of clutter issues, it's best to approach decluttering at a manageable rate to avoid a relapse

12. Thich Nhat Hanh, *Fragrant Palm Leaves: Journals, 1962–1966* (New York: Riverhead Trade, 1999), 173.

of bringing more stuff into the home. This is similar to someone losing a lot of weight and then gaining it all back plus more because the underlying reason for the weight hasn't been worked through. The root issue, which is inevitably resisting the loss of an old identity or the harboring of toxic emotions, must be brought into awareness. Seeing the past through tangible objects while decluttering is a powerful way to uproot and work through unresolved wounds and grief once and for all.

Collections

Collections can signal a holding on to something unfulfilled from the past. Sometimes they are simply an expression of one's passion, but they can also be a crying out of a long-held passion, identity, or belief that was never completely fulfilled or healed. In other words, they are an outer expression of an inner conflict. You might think you collect Santa Clauses because you like Santa Clauses. But there's usually a deeper reason why we collect what we collect.

For some, it could be a bolstering of a known identity. For example, my dad collected antique apothecary memorabilia that he displayed in his pharmacy. His desire to be a pharmacist was lived out, and the collection simply enhanced that identity and passion. Perhaps it was an identity that he knew would make his dad proud, and he therefore enhanced it through physical items.

For most people it is the subconscious mind's attempt to bring balance to some aspect of one's self. In *Memories, Dreams, Reflections*, Carl Jung describes it best: "Everything in the unconscious seeks outward manifestation, and the personality too desires to evolve out of its unconscious conditions and to experience itself as a whole." [13] A collection is an attempt to make the subconscious conscious. The more unconscious the underlying identity or emotional attachment, the more the collection will grow.

---

13. Carl Jung, *Memories, Dreams, Reflections* (New York: Vintage, 1965), 3.

In extreme cases, collections can completely run someone's life like an addiction, causing them to seek out the next item to add to the collection. Collections can also be costly, not to mention the sheer amount of space they take up. For these reasons, they can sometimes cause riffs in relationships or in cohabitation. Of course, they can also bring couples together if the two people share a common interest in the collection, which means they also share a similar underlying reason for collecting. The collection is like a child that they can pour their energy into and serves as a bond that keeps them together.

Collections often relate to an unhealed childhood wound. For example, collecting baseball cards could represent the desire to have played professional baseball or some other sport. But it more likely relates to the desire to be acknowledged or to be seen as a winner or even a hero. There is a lack of self-validation for which the baseball cards fill in the gap. Whatever the collectors find interesting or exciting about the collection is a shadow aspect of themselves.

Collecting dolls could be an expression for the desire for more nurturing. A Santa Claus collection could represent the unconscious desire to have had children or a specific association with holidays growing up. Sometimes the collection may relate to a past relative, and perhaps the collection is not even an expression of your personal desire but is one that you've inherited. If awareness is brought to the underlying reason or desire fueling the collection, then there can be resolve and more freedom around it.

Even past-life influences could be expressed through collections. This may account for the attraction to certain novelties that don't otherwise make sense to you. More likely though, it's a representation of something buried within one's subconscious that's at play in this life. On one of our family vacations, my mom decided she would start collecting matchbooks and shot glasses. This is funny, looking back, since she didn't drink or smoke. Perhaps it was a subconscious desire to be rebellious. She also had a lot of fire energy that she was not fully embodying in her life for which the matches could have been an outward expression.

If you decide you no longer want to continue a collection or feel like you need to reduce the collection, then you've probably moved through some of the underlying influences for the collection or found another outlet for the energy. For example, if you suddenly decide to sell your baseball card collection, perhaps you have found recent success in business or a more current interest that you are more passionate about. The baseball cards don't hold the same intrigue they once did. I had one client who decided it was time to trim down his gun collection. Guns were a prominent part of his identity as a hunter and fisherman. But as his interests shifted to more creative pursuits, he was feeling a desire to lighten his load by trading guns for pen and paper.

Comfort Items

There are some items we keep around simply out of comfort. Comfort items keep us grounded, soothe us in difficult times, or simply remind us who we are in the world. They can provide great benefit during difficult times. Think about when someone is in the hospital—having items from home bring great comfort. David Richo, in his book *When the Past Is Present*, refers to such items as a "transitional object." A blanket or teddy bear becomes "a metaphor for caring and safety."[14] With these items at hand we feel an extra sense of safety.

Transitional items are not just used by children. In adulthood, we use certain items to feel a sense of safety. It could be a special necklace, photo, or even a gemstone you keep in your pocket. When I placed all my belongings in storage except for two suitcases over a four-month period, it was interesting to observe what items I packed with me aside from essentials—my favorite crystals, a few books,

---

14. David Richo, *When the Past Is Present: Healing the Emotional Wounds That Sabotage Our Relationships* (Boston: Shambhala, 2008), 59.

and my angel card deck. I suppose these items gave me a sense of divine protection during such a tumultuous time.

Comfort items can also keep us stuck in the past if we rely on them like a security blanket providing us with so much comfort that we can't move forward. I see this often when women have teddy bears on their bed. I have observed this to be a major hindrance to attracting a relationship. However, if one is going through a time of great healing, then the teddy bear may bring needed comfort and security.

According to Richo, "Problems arise only when things are seen as magical or as substitutes for our own commitment to taking action in a way that would enable us to face our predicament in adult ways." [15] The question is whether an item empowers you or disempowers you. Is it a security blanket that's weighing you down or giving you a magic carpet ride?

How Decluttering Differs for Men and Women

After working with hundreds of clients, I started noticing a pattern of how men and women differ when it comes to their stuff and decluttering. What I observed is a generalization with exceptions and also doesn't take into account same-sex couples. But in general, men have more difficulty getting rid of clutter than women. That's not to say that women find decluttering easy, because they don't. In fact, women often blame much of their clutter issues on their husband. So before you give me a high five for calling out your spouse, read chapter 8, where I address the common excuses of passing the blame on to others.

The reason men tend to have more difficulty in letting go of items from the past is because they generally do not process emotions as easily as women. As you can see from the preceding chapters, our stuff encapsulates our emotions, making the process of decluttering

---

15. Ibid., 60.

essentially a process of releasing emotional weight and grieving the past. It's much more than a physical task of placing items in a bag.

This makes decluttering no easy feat for those who are not in touch with their emotions—men or women. When someone is not in tune with their emotions, their possessions are more likely to become memory keepers of the past. This is why the slightest mention of getting rid of something from the past can be met with great resistance. You might as well have suggested they amputate their left leg, when it's just a college sweatshirt.

Men tend to hang on to mementos relating to their identity from their early days of feeling free prior to settling down with marriage and children. They may also be drawn to keeping items relating to family heritage and legacy as it relates to successes. Women, on the other hand, tend to identify more with their close relationships. This is simply a reflection of the thousands of years in which men were the hunters and women were the nurturers.

Men are more likely to externally display their prized possessions from the past, such as a deer head, diploma, or signed football. Women, on the other hand, tend to hold their personal possessions closer and stored more internally in jewelry boxes, photo albums, or journals tucked away in a closet. In either case, the more the past is present—whether displayed or stored—the more it is clutter if it's preventing you from moving forward.

If your spouse's clutter is giving you fits, you probably already know that nagging them about it doesn't work. In fact, it might just spin them into acting like an eight-year-old child again with their mother telling them to clean their room. That gets old quick. The best and, really, only way to inspire your spouse (or anyone in the world) to do anything is to be the example yourself.

I've seen this approach work time and time again in households. Decluttering is contagious. If you start the process, others in your household will join in. As you lighten your load, it causes an energetic shift in the house. They will either join forces with you or revolt more. But revolting will eventually take too much energy to maintain and surrender will happen. It's pretty magical. Give it a try.

CHAPTER 7

Too Much of a Good Thing
Overcompensation of Identity

Up to this point, you've read about how the past is largely responsible for why we hang on to stuff and how it keeps us stuck. Items associated with past identities usually go unused for some time or stored away completely out of sight. But what about the stuff in your current life? Is it still too much? Is a clutter intervention needed for items in your everyday life?

Most of us have a strong affinity toward certain types of items. You can call it your Achilles' heel of clutter. There's no harm, no foul in indulging in items we enjoy until and unless it becomes too much of a good thing. When this happens, things we love end up causing us distress. Before reading on, you probably already have an idea of what those items are for you. I've always loved shopping for clothes. For other people, it may be bath products, magazines, or shoes. Why do we gravitate toward certain items over others, and when is it too much?

In the following sections, you may recognize yourself as being prone to having an overabundance of the types of items mentioned.

If you feel like the amount is problematic for you, then it's time to take a closer look at those areas. The items we possess should enhance our energy, not deplete it. Too much of a good thing can turn in on itself and become a source of stress.

The items we possess should enhance our energy, not deplete it. Too much of good thing can turn in on itself and become a source of stress.

The law of diminishing marginal utility can be applied to our stuff. According to this economic theory, the first bite of ice cream tastes amazing. But the enjoyment wanes with each successive bite. And then if you eat too much of it, you actually feel sick. This applies to our stuff too. What started out as something enjoyable ends up depleting your energy. This happens with the items in our home, especially those items we love the most. And yet you must consider why you in effect "overeat" that particular item to the point where it has diminishing utility for you.

For example, if you love magazines and have a lot of magazines, by all means enjoy your magazines. However, if it gets to the point where they add more stress to your life than benefit, then it's time to consider why you have collected beyond what feels good to you. If it's a source of constant decluttering and you feel like it overtakes you in some way, then it's a sign that there's more going on than meets the eye.

When we feel like we've hit our max with certain items, it's usually because we've run out of space for it in our home, which also means it's overtaking our energy in our life as well. When we run out of space in our home, it's a clue that we have allowed something to overtake our time, our energy, and our boundaries in some way. Our home space is a literal metaphor for our personal energetic space.

Think of your home as an external second layer of your energy field. The size of your home is representative of how much space you energetically take up. This is one of the fears I have with people seeking the trendy tiny house movement. It is attractive to those people who are seeking to take up less space on the planet, but paradoxically it could come at the cost of one's own abundance and the positive impact they can make in the world. However, it can be a great benefit for those who wouldn't otherwise occupy a space of their own or who have ample social outlets outside their home.

I find that most people have one of two problems: not enough space or too much space. Our square footage shrinks or expands in correlation with certain phases of our life. It's common for people to downsize with retirement or after grown kids have left the nest. There is no longer a desire to take up as much space in the world and instead a desire to live more simply. This is also reflected in owning fewer items.

On the other hand, couples often move into larger spaces upon getting married, usually with the desire to expand into a family. This expansion can also lend to marriages falling apart if the couple is not able to embody the larger space that is required of them. If there is a lot of empty space in the home, then there is a lot of empty space in the marriage, which makes it ripe for other energies coming into the marriage.

When we run out of space in our home, it's a clue that we have allowed something to overtake our time, our energy, and our boundaries in some way.

If you feel like your home is too small for the items you want to possess, then perhaps it is. If this is the case, you will move into a larger space. If that isn't feasible, then you won't. I know that's a simplistic way of viewing it, but the size of your home is in alignment with your current energy until it's not, and that's when you will move. Whether you want to upsize, downsize, or stay where you are, if your belongings are taking over your space to the point where you feel uncomfortable in your space, then it's time to declutter.

Understanding the underlying reason you are drawn to certain items will give you the necessary motivation to declutter that area of your life. Otherwise, it will feel like an unending uphill battle of constantly clearing out magazines, or papers, or clothing, or whatever your Achilles' heel of clutter is with no real relief.

Anytime we grip too tightly or hoard something, we end up with what we fear the most. Life is meant to be an organic inflow and outflow.

Each section below highlights common items and the identity surrounding those items. Each identity also has a shadow side. This is what's really playing out if you have an overabundance of that type of item. The shadow side of any identity is what we fear the most, and so we overcompensate to avoid it. As a result, what we fear is exactly what ends up happening. Anytime we grip too tightly or hoard something, we end up with what we fear the most. Life is meant to be an organic inflow and outflow. This allows fresh energy to circulate in our life. Whenever we have an excess of one thing, it's an overcompensation for something else. Simply acknowledging it is usually enough to bring the imbalance into balance. Let's take a closer look at each of these and see where your clutter intervention needs to take place.

Beauty Products: The Beauty Queen

Are your cabinets cluttered with beauty products? From makeup that was the wrong color, to facial creams that didn't smell good, to hair conditioners that made hair frizzy, to skin toners that dried out the skin, to travel shampoos that might be needed one day? These are usually stashed in bathroom cabinets and finally get our attention when we run out of space or upon moving.

What is it about beauty products that makes them so hard to throw away?

There's almost a whole bottle left.

I might still use it.

I could refill my travel bottles with it.

I could use it for travel.

Even though it made my skin break out, it might not the next time I try it.

It was expensive.

I don't want to waste it.

I should give it to my sister.

The excuses for hanging on to these products run the gamut. Believe it or not, all of those are cover excuses for what's really going on.

Most females use beauty products of some sort, but women whose identities are strongly associated with their appearance are more likely to have more beauty products. Whatever we focus on we get more of. If your appearance has been an asset or a positive part of your identity, then you are more likely to spend more time and money on that area of life. This is true regardless of whether you believe you are pretty or not.

This is common for women who were positively acknowledged in some way for their appearance, such as being voted homecoming queen, working as a model, or simply being favored by guys. The attention puts more of a focus on this area of their life, positively or negatively. Often in families, siblings are known for either their brains or beauty. I had one friend whose role in the family was to "just sit there and look pretty."

When one's entire identity is wrapped around appearance, or anything for that matter, insecurity can easily rear its head. This is especially true as one gets older and looks begin to fade, at least in terms of societal standards.

If I lose my looks, who am I then?

Who am I if I'm not the beauty queen?

What happens when I no longer look attractive?

These are the subconscious fears that lend to purchasing and subsequently holding on to beauty products even if not used.

In an attempt to hold on to our beauty, we hold on to beauty products. Obviously, there is no logical correlation to this. There is no way that the more beauty products we possess, the less likely it is for our appearance to slip away. But energetically, holding on to these items is an outward manifestation of the desire to hold on to one's beauty or an endless attempt to perfect it. There is an irrational subconscious belief that by simply possessing these products, even if unused, one's appearance will be maintained or perhaps even improved.

While treating skin, hair, and nails is important to maintaining or enhancing one's beauty, the amount of products used for this is inconsequential. Think quality, not quantity. Be okay with letting a product go if it didn't perform the way you had hoped. If you feel guilt or shame for wasting money on something you have to throw away, then you were probably shamed in some way with regard to your appearance growing up.

Consider your language around your resistance to tossing these items: *waste, guilty, frivolous, it's a shame, down the tubes.* These are indicative of your energy around your appearance and self-care, most likely based on past programming from childhood. Be aware if these are still thoughts that feel true to you. Most likely you have moved past it consciously but are still being influenced by others from your past. Simply identify what you truly believe and make a decision from that place. Know that loosening your grip on extraneous beauty products will allow more space for your true beauty to shine.

Papers, Magazines, and Ideas: The Resourceful

If beauty products aren't your thing, then maybe piles of papers, magazines, or books are. Papers can come in the form of mail, household papers, magazines, notes, to-do-lists, books, or any other resource on paper. You know who you are if this section applies to you. It's a never-ending stack of papers to be dealt with. I have one friend who is always tackling an unending stack of "paperwork" despite her simplistic lifestyle.

My dad also falls into this category. He doesn't throw any information away. Everything is "to be filed," except there are no files—just stacks of paper everywhere. He usually has a couple of news articles or phone numbers stuffed in his pocket to give someone. Instead of a smartphone, he has smart pockets. He is resourceful and knows some really random stuff, some of which is quite useful. I use him as an example of someone whose identity is that of being resourceful. They pride themselves on having information at their fingertips, literally.

For these information junkies, being resourceful is very much a part of their identity. It's where they feel valuable and helpful to the world and derive self-worth. They enjoy the exchange of information on the mental level—learning it for themselves or sharing it with others, usually both. The idea of getting rid of these information resources feels preposterous to them.

The information at issue may also pertain to one's work. Chapter 4 discussed papers and manuals as they relate to one's past job or career, but it may also relate to one's current work. Many artists collect a plethora of papers that are stashed away for ideas, whether for visual inspiration or literal application. I had one client who did scrapbook art. Her entire office was about to explode with pieces of paper and she couldn't figure out why she felt stuck in her work. There was such an overabundance of inspirational papers that there was no room for creativity to squeeze in.

Papers are certainly valuable, but when do they become too much of a good thing? You most likely know when you are up to your ears in too much paper. People with too much paper are rarely in denial that they've exceeded their threshold. When they have too much paper, it impedes their resourcefulness. There's a desire to lighten their load, but fear swoops in.

What if I throw something useful away?

What if I need it later?

Am I throwing away a good idea?

I might need that for a future project.

My client might need it.

The excuses for keeping information run wild. And suddenly these information junkies are stopped in their tracks, feeling paralyzed by the thought of discarding a sliver of paper. When feeling overwhelmed, making logical decisions is impossible. When this is the case, then there's something else at play. The fear that represents the shadow side of being resourceful is feeling out of the loop. This frightens anyone whose identity is based in resourcefulness, even if they are not aware of it.

If this feels all too familiar for you, simply acknowledge that information gathering and sharing is a part of who you are. If it is transacted through your work or art, acknowledge that as well. This is an aspect of you that can't be taken away even if every scrap of paper, magazine article, or news clipping were erased from your home or deleted from your hard drive. Life will always bring new and fresh information to you. Resourceful people fear being out of the loop so much that they hang on to paper and information to the point of stagnation. As a result, they lose their resourcefulness—exactly what they fear.

For information junkies, I recommend a gradual process of letting information go. In freeing the physical space of paper, you are freeing aspects of your mind as well. This will allow new ideas and thoughts to come in. Information lives on the mental level, which is why too much of it can cloud our mental faculties. This is also why having too much paper can also be a subconscious distraction tactic and is linked to procrastination.

Procrastination is a byproduct of fear. We fear what it means to be actually successful and how the resulting changes would affect us. By nature, no one is a procrastinator. Our soul is always driven toward something. Fear is what resists that flow. Having stacks of papers to tackle keeps one in distraction mode, where procrastination thrives. If this applies to you, I recommend rereading the section on "The Fear of Empty Space" in chapter 1. What are you really afraid of? The more you can acknowledge it and bring it to the light, the less it will be a hidden force running the show.

Clothing: The Stylish

Many women can relate to feeling like they have too many clothes. This category seems to trigger the common *just in case* excuse, which is discussed at length in the next chapter. Clothing is the closest and most personal representation of our identity. When we keep clothing items just in case we might need them in the future, it's almost always a sign that we haven't quite given up a former identity. We keep those items around just in case we might need to revert back to that person again one day.

Like wearing a "different hat," we keep certain clothing items or outfits in the back of our closet just in case we need to fit into a certain role at some point. It's almost like a costume closet of all our different personalities. Within our current life, we have a variety of personas and personalities that we play out—the lazy weekend person, the professional person, the party person, and so on.

Be honest about what roles you want to continue playing. Do you trust who you are now? Do you accept who you are now? Or are you keeping some old identities around just in case this one doesn't pan out? This could be anything from a skinnier version of yourself to being a corporate banker. Decluttering clothes related to past jobs and careers is discussed in chapter 4, but what about clothing items that relate to the present?

If you feel like an overabundance of clothing is your Achilles' heel, then you most likely enjoy being stylish. Clothing can certainly serve a utilitarian purpose, but those who have an overabundance of clothing usually have an identity around being stylish with an underlying fear of being outdated. If that's true, then why would a stylish person keep out-of-style clothes in their closet?

Being stylish comes with a price tag. Trending through clothes can get expensive. Spending money on an outfit you wore once to a party, or maybe even never at all, comes with an even higher price tag: guilt. Guilt is a common emotion that hijacks our natural process of letting go. Realizing you don't like the black-and-white striped shirt should be an easy giveaway. That is, until guilt rears its head.

Guilt can rationalize anything. The next thing you know you are wearing that shirt to work and feeling awful all day. Or maybe you stuff the shirt in the back of your closet and to try to forget that you spent $59.99 on it. Nice try. Guilt is guilt. You can't stuff it away in a bag in the back of a closet. In fact, that's when guilt turns into shame. Shame thrives when sequestered away in secretive hiding places.

There's something extra guilt-inducing about spending money on ourselves. The paradox is that if the guilt is active in one's vibration, then it will continue to show up. You will make an ill-advised purchase with that blouse sitting in your closet, drenched in guilt and with the price tag still attached. This is what ultimately leads to your closet becoming stuffed with items you never wear and you wondering why you have such a hard time getting rid of them. You are a vibrational match to the energy of guilt.

Instead, acknowledge that you enjoy being stylish. Own this as something you enjoy. Think of it as a hobby. Be okay with gambling on a dress you might only wear once to a special occasion. Own the fact that you don't want to feel outdated. You enjoy feeling current and trendy. Start to let go of items you truly know you will never wear—even if they still have the price tags. Donate them to an organization that you feel makes a positive contribution to its community. This will ease the guilt and help shift you into a place of freedom. Shopping will become less impulsive, and you will start to love and wear everything in your closet.

Status Symbols: The Successful

We usually think of clutter as items with little or no value, but there is no price tag on clutter. Clutter can be a million-dollar Picasso painting. Clutter is anything that's no longer in your highest and best interest to keep. It's anything that you no longer love or use. For example, if a Picasso painting was given to you by a former partner who verbally abused you, then it's clutter. The energy around it is not serving you. You can see how clutter doesn't always mean a massive quantity of stuff. It also refers to the quality of the energy it holds for you.

> We usually think of clutter
> as items with little or no value,
> but there is no price tag on clutter.

There's no problem with owning expensive items. We came into a physical existence for the purpose of experiencing the physical world and its abundance in the form of material objects. However, when people hang on to expensive items even after they've outworn the items' usefulness or exceeded their bank account, it's usually the result of the desire to feel successful.

Feeling successful is a positive virtue, but too much of a good thing may be an overcompensation for an insecurity of feeling like a failure. This could be the result of having grown up in meager living conditions. Later in life, when success and money are achieved, there is a splurge on material items of which the person was once deprived. The items are evidence of their success and say to the world, "I am successful."

Again, there is no judgment on enjoying the material pleasures in life. However, if it gets to the point of causing more harm than good, then it's too much. That could be spending beyond one's means, having too much inventory of cars or homes to maintain, or becoming completely consumed in the materiality of life to the point where any sense of spirituality is lost. This is when the American dream becomes a nightmare.

Luxury items or status symbols could be in the form of cars, jewelry, artwork, or high-end designer brands. If this resonates with you, then simply acknowledge that you are successful. Acknowledge that you or your work adds value to the world. The more you own this yourself, the less you'll need to own external items outside of yourself to prove this. You can adopt a "less is more" mentality in which each item is loved, used, and appreciated.

Children's Toys: The Good Mother

The "less is more" mentality also applies to children's toys. A British researcher found that the average ten-year-old has 238 toys and only plays with approximately twelve of them on a daily basis.[16] You've most likely watched a child play with a set of keys much longer than a sophisticated kids' toy purchased to stimulate the child's mind. Kids don't need a huge number of toys to be happy or from which to learn.

Even with fewer toys, there's no doubt that it's harder to keep a home orderly and clutter free when there are kids involved. And yet studies also show that children prefer an orderly environment. Order gives children a sense of structure. And structure equates to safety. Even if they enjoy spreading toys around the house, that doesn't mean it's their preference. Being messy is just their temporary way of understanding the physical world. It's the parents' job to teach the children to pick up after themselves when they reach the appropriate age. Organization is a learned skill, and emulating what their caregivers do is a big part of the learning process. The phrase "Do as I say, not as I do" doesn't work for children. It must be organically demonstrated and positively affirmed.

If your home feels overrun by toys, determine if it's an organizational issue or a consumption issue. If it's just a matter of better organization, then the solution is simple. It may be as easy as teaching your child to put the toys back. If they are not old enough, then it's up to you to do that for the child. In some cases, it may be necessary to purchase more functional storage containers or furniture items to hold the toys.

If square footage is an issue, then the number of toys will need to be downsized. Our belongings can't take up more room than what's available. It's that simple. Trying to stuff more in a box than will fit is a direct path to stagnation, emotional claustrophobia, and feeling

---

16. "Ten-year-olds have £7,000 worth of toys but play with just £330," *The Telegraph*, October 20, 2010.

overwhelmed. It's the ultimate battle of the bulge. If this is the case, then your only option is to get rid of some toys.

Decluttering toys can be a little tricky because most kids don't like change. They may resist the desire to get rid of toys. After all, these toys were used to form the child's identity, and now they're being whisked away into a black hole. This is similar to the first time a child goes potty and is distraught that a part of them is being flushed down the toilet.

Some kids may not even notice that certain toys are gone, whereas other children will immediately notice a change in their room. If you are met with resistance from your child, it's important to explain the importance of letting items go. You can tell them they will go to other kids in need or whatever story you want to present. You know your child and what they'll best respond to. This is an important setup for a lifelong practice of adhering to the natural flow in life of letting go of things and allowing new things to come in.

If you struggle with giving in to your child's desire for more and more toys to the point where overpurchasing is the primary issue, then this presents a different challenge. It is natural for children to want things. Everything is new to them and ripe for exploration. But this doesn't mean you have to give in to it. When parents give in to the children's whims at the cost of having too much stuff, then they are overcompensating for not being a good enough parent.

Giving control over to the child to determine what comes into the house is also a boundary violation. This is more than just allowing your child to pick out a new toy. I'm referring to situations in which toys have overtaken the home. In this case, you've given your power over to your child. This is most likely a pattern that shows up in other areas of your life—the inability to say no in order to make others happy. If you start with your children's toys, the control issue will continue into the child's adolescence and even into adulthood in ways that come with a higher price.

Consider if you feel guilty in some aspect of being a mom. This can also apply to dads who aren't around as much as they'd like to be. We often use gifts or tangible objects as a replacement for time and attention. Do you feel like you're not giving your child enough of your time and so you attempt to replace this with toys? Or do you feel like you give and give and give and it's never enough? This is a common pattern of those who struggle with unworthiness. It's important to investigate the root of why you overgive to your child.

All transactions hold an energetic undercurrent. If unworthiness or guilt is at the root of your interaction with your child, that energy will get passed on. If there's some aspect of your parenting that you don't feel is adequate, clarify for yourself what that is. Is it legitimate? If so, what changes can you make? Or is it an unfounded pressure you're putting on yourself?

In many cases, simple organizing tips can give some order and structure to a home with kids and toys while also providing a space for play and creativity. With simple teaching moments, children will quickly pick up on organizing skills, which will benefit them for the rest of their lives. Here are some ways to maintain a sense of peace, balance, and order in the house without the accumulation of clutter:

Be the Example

Children learn by watching their caregivers. If you keep your personal spaces such as your bedroom clean, then your children will already have a leg up. If you are cleaning up, show your child what you are doing even to the point of narrating the process. Those who are clutter-prone usually had clutterbug parents, although this can vary among personality types too. It is possible to be messy and also learn to be organized. It's just a choice to implement or not.

Teach Your Child Organizational Skills

Organization doesn't come naturally for many people, just like drawing doesn't come naturally to everyone. But anything can be learned. There are hundreds of books on the topic. To set you and your child up for success, you must have the proper infrastructure in place. This usually starts in storage areas. For example, have or install adequate organization systems, such as shoe racks, sweater shelves, toy bins, and so on. Show them where their dirty clothes go, where stuffed animals go, and where board games go. Believe it or not, they want to know and will have a sense of accomplishment upon putting things in their place.

Budget in Cleanup Time

Make cleanup time a part of your child's playtime. For example, if they have an hour or two of playtime, dedicate the last five or ten minutes to cleaning up. This will carry over into all areas of their life for the rest of their life. Completing tasks is something most adults overlook. If learned at an early age, it will be easier later on.

Make It Fun

Clearing clutter does not have to be painful. In fact, I recommend turning on some good music and make it as enjoyable as possible. As for children, it's all about how you sell it. Make it fun, upbeat, and positive. Don't pass the negative attitude on to your child.

Explain the Bigger Picture

Clearing clutter can be a great teaching moment for children. Have them help you pack up toys and clothes they no longer use in order to donate to those less fortunate. Children are inherently kind-hearted and will enjoy this process. This will make it easier the next time and the next time until they automatically start collecting unused items themselves.

Designate a Place for Creativity

Providing a place for drawing, painting, and other forms of self-expression is important. In some cases, parents find these activities too messy and use schools as a forum instead. However, children oftentimes need the safety of expressing themselves at home without peer pressure. Art is a great way to keep an open line of communication between the parent and child. Allow them to use the kitchen or some other family space for doing homework. Designate a specific area in the house for these activities to create a sense of creative space. This will also help keep visual clutter at a minimum in the other areas of the home.

Allow Individuation

A child's bedroom is a haven for them to explore their identity, especially as they enter adolescence. If they are not able to adequately develop identity at this stage, then their development could be delayed, resulting in them not knowing who they are in adulthood. Allow adolescents to explore phases in their room by allowing them to personalize their space. This may be hanging posters or art, picking paint colors, or even selecting furniture. With appropriate parental discretion, allow them the freedom to move furniture around, to create spaces within a space, such as a fort, or even to decorate their own space.

Part of identity development for children is to have a private space where they can be alone when needed. This can be as nurturing as family time and helps them set boundaries later on in relationships. If you are not sure what is "normal" during this phase, contact a child therapist to get more information. Oftentimes during the identity formation phase, children or adolescents can become quite messy. Encourage them to clean their space. Use reward systems and positive incentives. A clean space will help them with homework and help them see solutions to problems much more clearly.

Messy Environment: The Creative

Instead of priding themselves on having a neat environment, some people wrap their identity around having a messy environment. In the same way people talk about how dramatic their life is or what a "train wreck" they are, having a messy home gives them an identity as well. Creative types or artists might also tout their messy space as a way to validate themselves as a true artist. I commend someone for not having shame for keeping their home messy, but it could be inhibiting their creative process instead of contributing to it.

There can certainly be positives to a messy environment as opposed to an overly structured environment, which is discussed in the next section. Many artists find that the lack of structure enriches their creativity. This is the same reason kids like to be messy when playing. It is their creativity at work. Of course, learning order is important too. Messy is intuitive; controlled is analytical. Is the space a product of the mind, or is the mind a product of the space? I believe it goes both ways. You can be creative and find structure. In fact, it's essential. The more structure you have, the more creative you can be. This is the yin and yang of the creative process and is well illustrated by professional dancers.

Dancer and author Twyla Tharp writes about the combination of these opposing forces and how they contribute to the creative process in her book *The Creative Habit*. Dancers embody the fluidity of dance in tandem with the necessary structure. Their structure consists not only of their muscular framework, but also of their dedication and discipline to the practice. This is the case with any artistry. You don't have to be messy to be a great artist. In fact, I would take it one step further and say you can be an even greater artist by bringing more structure into your environment.

For creative types, much of the messy environment consists of inspirations, from nature to paper to paints to pictures. But over time, enough is enough and our stuff starts to dampen the creative process. We all have a different standard of what is too messy or too much clutter. You know when your home or studio has gotten out of control. You feel scattered, cloudy, weighed down, or creatively stuck. That's when you know it's time to take action. Here are some tips to integrate structure into your creative world:

Designate Space

The size of your studio space will ultimately dictate how much art and supplies you can have on hand. When it comes to art, you can fill a warehouse space just as easy as you could fill a small corner of the kitchen. The first step is to designate how much space you are willing and wanting to take up.

Organize

If you don't already have proper storage, then consider purchasing organizing units available at any art supply or office store. Have proper storage and organization in your designated space so that you will at least have a standard for organization and have a place for everything. This way you will know when your space has gotten too messy for even your right brain.

Downsize

If you have too much stuff to fit into your organizing units, then it's time to downsize. This is where the emotional aspects come into play—they'll help you decide what to keep and what not to keep. If you keep items for inspiration, such as photos, cards, and images, then go through them to see what still resonates with you. You may be surprised how different you feel about some of the items. After all, our art evolves as we do. Discard any items that no longer inspire you.

Stay Current

What to do with your past projects can be quite challenging for artists. It took me several years and several purges to finally dispose of my interior design projects. I kept what I needed to create a portfolio. For boards that I knew I would never need or use again, I took pictures of them before eventually disposing of them. It was difficult knowing how much time had gone into them. But honestly, I haven't missed them since. In fact, I felt much lighter once I got rid of them. And it allowed room for new creativity in my life.

When your designated space for past projects starts to overflow, it's time to determine what needs to go. I periodically dispose of my pieces of art that aren't, well, that great. Taking pictures of your work is a great way to track your progress without being overloaded with projects. Clearing out old projects will also make room for new ideas and creativity. Don't get too weighed down in your past projects and instead let creativity flow through you and your studio.

Neat Environment: The Organizer

Some people pride themselves on being messy, while others tout having a neat and tidy space. When taken to the extreme, either can be equally detrimental to finding balance. I grew up in an overly neat home. It was organized, structured, and controlled. I learned organization, which taught me discipline and order in my work, but it also left little room for spontaneity, creativity, and play. In an overly tidy environment, the analytical left brain is fully in charge, preventing the emotional right brain from developing.

In working with clients, I find that overly neat people are less likely to see or admit to their personal challenges, which makes adapting to change more difficult. In fact, there may be a strong identity around having it all together and maintaining a perfect life. An overly neat space is indicative of control issues and a lack of spontaneity. It's also a sign of strict boundaries with other people. Not surprisingly, the space can come between relationships because of the person's strong desire for control and organization.

Just like you can't tell a messy person
to suddenly become organized,
you also can't tell an organized person
to suddenly become messy.

Just like you can't tell a messy person to suddenly become organized, you also can't tell an organized person to suddenly become messy. It's been a part of their core identity for most of their life and a byproduct of how they run their energy in general. No self-help or decluttering book is going to change someone overnight. The change has to take place on the inside first, which starts with a desire to change, or at least the desire for a more balanced life or more creativity.

If you decide you would prefer less structure and wish to embrace a more creative life, then working with your home is a great place to start. It's not so much about getting less organized as it is noticing what drives your desire for organization. Notice what emotions come up when you see the dishes in the sink. Catch yourself in the moment. Notice your desire for order. At the root is the feeling of having no control in your life.

Organizing is a way of exerting control. The paradox is that those who are the most organized actually feel the most out of control. Their tidy environment gives them a sense of being in control of their world. But it also covers the pain of feeling out of control. This could mean not living the life you want to be living or being in a life you don't want to be in. It's a way to mask the pain so no one will notice, including yourself.

In the same way the overly messy person distracts their emotions with stuff, the overly neat person tricks everyone, including themselves, into thinking they live the perfect life. They may even pride themselves on being clutter free. If this feels like you, try leaving items sitting out more often than usual. This may not be a permanent desire for your home environment, but it may trigger the underlying emotions that are really at issue.

If you're overly neat, then you might think you're off the hook when it comes to decluttering. You're not. Just because your closets are organized doesn't mean there's not stuff in there that's keeping you stuck. It just means your stuff is properly folded and correctly labeled. And you've probably been that much more strategic in storing and organizing your clutter out of sight.

Those with overly neat homes may also have the opposite problems of clutterbugs, and that's getting rid of too much. I occasionally have clients whose homes are sparse and void of any personality. You may know someone like this. When you go to their home, it feels stark and cold. Releasing too much is as much of an issue as holding on to too much. Balance is the key. The goal of a clutter intervention is not to achieve minimalism necessarily, but instead to create a supportive environment for you and your family.

CHAPTER 8

To Keep or Not to Keep
Common Cover Excuses

From the preceding chapters, you can see there's usually more to the decluttering process than just putting items in a bag. With more understanding of why we hold on to certain items, we can let them go with more ease. However, sometimes there's one more mental hoop to jump through. Our ego can get the best of us and trick us into holding on to the past. Just when you're about to get rid of the broken toaster, your mind starts questioning the decision.

Maybe I can get it fixed.

Maybe someone can use the parts.

Maybe my neighbor wants it.

What seems like an easy task of cleaning out your closet leads to a mind full of dialogue.

I might need this just in case.

What if my kids want it one day?

It feels like a waste to just give it away.

These are all common excuses I've heard time and time again from clients. You may have even read about these in other decluttering books and resources. But I'm here to tell you that these excuses are actually just cover excuses for something even deeper. The good news is we all use them and they can easily be debunked.

If you're still struggling with an item, you may hear one of these excuses running through your head. Even if you're aware that it's just an excuse and mentally wrestle it to the ground, you're still not sure what to do. In order to take clear action, you have to get to the root of what's really at play. At the bottom of each one of these common excuses is a deeper truth.

One of the most common emotions triggered in the decluttering process is guilt. If we're holding on to any guilt, it will certainly rear its head before an item heads to the giveaway bag or trash can, especially if it was a gift. Other common excuses run the gamut from saving items for kids to saving the planet to *just in case* just-about-anything-you-can-think-of.

If you've read up to this point and you're still struggling with some items, then this chapter is for you. You've most likely encountered one or more of the following cover excuses that your ego creatively comes up with to keep you in the past, where your comfort zone lies. You will see what they all have in common is that they're simply distracting you from the real issue of hanging on to an old identity or unresolved emotions from your past, as covered in previous chapters.

It Was a Gift

What to do with unwanted gifts is one of the most difficult decisions we face when decluttering. For this reason, getting rid of them is one of the most transformational things you can do to declutter. For gifts relating to past romantic relationships, I recommend referring to chapter 3 for how to handle those items.

I was recently at a client's home helping her declutter. When I asked her about certain items that energetically registered as clutter, she would explain that they were a gift from someone. I began to wonder if I don't receive a lot of gifts or whether I give away my gifts. I realized that we attract what we value. She values physical items, whereas I value experiences. We all have a different preference for how much stuff we enjoy having. This particular client genuinely liked all her stuff (or most of it), but she admitted it was too much. This is where prioritization comes into play. We must prioritize our favorites. An unwanted gift doesn't have to mean you don't like the item per se but that you just don't have space for it.

What about gifts we know we don't want but feel an obligation to keep? Therein lies the struggle. We usually do one of three things with unwanted gifts: stuff them in a closet and worry about them later, display them reluctantly, or keep them hidden until the gift giver comes to visit. The excuse we use is that we don't want to hurt the other person's feelings. But I'm going to challenge you. It's actually you avoiding your own feelings. The gift excuse is masking guilt and your reluctance to giving it away is your avoidance of feeling the guilt.

For most people, receiving is more difficult than giving because it triggers our self-worth. We usually aren't concerned with what people do with gifts we give, just the gifts we receive. When we give a gift, we feel good about what we've done and move on. When we receive a gift, however, we have to feel worthy of the gift. And so when it comes time to get rid of it, our guilt consciousness is triggered.

Not only was receiving this gift hard, but now I'm wanting to get rid of it. What kind of person am I?

What if she finds out I got rid of it? She'll think I'm not a good friend. That would be horrible. I am horrible.

He'll think I'm ungrateful and a selfish person. I probably am ungrateful and selfish.

These are some of the conversations we have with ourselves, either consciously or unconsciously. If you can pinpoint your exact words in the story you tell yourself, it will give you clues to what's really at the root of your beliefs about yourself. *Ungrateful. Selfish. Not loyal. Horrible.* No wonder getting rid of these items is so difficult. It triggers us at our core wounds. Shame lies beneath guilt, and underneath shame is the lack of self-worth. All those emotions get triggered from a seemingly innocent twenty-dollar birthday gift.

When self-worth wounds are triggered, a domino effect of boundary issues in our life begins. The lower our self-esteem, the more likely we are to allow our boundaries to be crossed. Having items in our home that we don't like or want represents a boundary we've allowed to be crossed. This includes unwanted gifts. You should love every item in your home, whether it is in your closet or sitting out.

Having items in our home that we don't
like or want represents a boundary
we've allowed to be crossed.

The exception to this rule is items of others with whom you co-habitate in the home or items about which you've agreed to compromise. Although, if you find yourself compromising to the point of having no voice or no space of your own, then this is also a boundary crossing. The belongings in the home are representative of a bigger picture of yourself and your relationships.

Most of us grew up with our boundaries or preferences violated, and thus this feels familiar. In fact, we might have received shame when we attempted to stand our ground. Maybe you received a doll for Christmas that you weren't that into. Let's say your response wasn't exactly joyous. You may have heard language like "You need to be grateful for what you get" or "Beggars can't be choosers" or "Tell Grandma how much you love the gift."

As children, most of us didn't have a lot of choices about what we wore, what we ate, and what we played with. What our parents provided for us was our definition of being taken care of and therefore what we perceived as love. This has changed to some degree in recent years in parenting styles in which children are given more freedom of choice. But even so, there is inevitably some filtering from the caregiver. We got used to others' preferences being imposed upon us. Resisting them just led to shame so we learned to give in and put a smile on our face. This pattern may still be alive and well within you. It's important to end it and make your preferences a priority.

Getting rid of unwanted gifts also includes unwanted inherited items. There is no reason to continue passing down guilt through your family tree. Trust me, your deceased relatives will understand. It is your own emotional tie, not theirs. Surround yourself only with items and furniture that you love, that resonate with you, and that enhance your daily life. Once you stop holding on to unwanted gifts, you will stop the barrage of them coming to you. And you'll most likely start receiving *wanted* gifts.

Stuffing an unwanted item in the closet is the same as stuffing guilt. At the same time, displaying an unwanted item is a daily reminder of what that gift represents. The only answer is to get rid of unwanted gifts. If this is too difficult, then pledge to keep the item for one year and then give it away.

Be mindful of what gifts you give people and if you have expectations or conditions with which you are giving the gift. Give gifts you think the person truly wants, not what you want for them. Be nonattached from there. Give from your heart unconditionally. If you're unsure what someone wants, then give an intangible gift such as a service, an experience, something consumable, or a gift card.

Just in Case

This is the most popular of all decluttering excuses. This is our default, easy go-to when all else fails. *What if I need it later?* What if you do need it later? Is it really the end of the world? I'll be honest, I've gotten rid of some items that I kind of wish I hadn't. I've looked for something, couldn't find it, and then remembered, "Oh, shoot, I gave that away." I struggle with a balance of hanging on to too much and getting rid of too much. And while I admit there are some items I probably could have used later, I actually don't regret giving them away. The benefit of getting rid of too much has definitely outweighed hanging on to too much.

The *just in case* excuse is most often used by those who tend toward feeling a sense of lack instead of abundance. This excuse is especially activated with items that may still have functional value. For those who experienced the Depression era or other financial hardships earlier in life, material items were not plentiful and conservation meant survival. It's understandable that this would still be an active consideration, even if subconscious, when processing items. Due to the mass production of material goods, those who grew up in the 1940s saw a starkly different amount of consumer goods than those who grew up in the 1980s.

Regardless of the amount of money and material possessions you have, it's important to recognize if you are operating under a mindset of lack. A millionaire can feel lack while an artist living month-to-month can feel abundant. In the case of the millionaire, even though present needs are met, if not exceeded, there is always a fear lurking that it could all be lost, whereas the artist believes one day her paintings will go for thousands of dollars and enjoys her days painting. In both cases, the underlying thought will most likely become true.

Another consideration is if you are keeping an item just in case of a negative event that's within your control. A common example of this is keeping your "fat clothes" in case you gain weight again. Your weight is within your control. Keeping the fat clothes is simply setting this scenario up to become true. That being said, if your weight tends to fluctuate and you're okay with it, then perhaps it makes sense to keep a variety of sizes on hand.

Compare this to keeping items for situations outside of our control, such as natural disasters or emergency situations. You may want to keep a snow shovel, a generator, a tire pump, a first-aid kit, or other functional items that come in handy just in case of an emergency.

If you are using the *just in case* excuse when decluttering, consider the worst-case scenario: you have to repurchase the item. If that happens, chances are you'll want to purchase a different and better version of that item. We are always expanding, and rarely do we want to repeat the past.

Let's say at stake is a pair of ragged jeans you hadn't worn in years. They still have some life in them although they fit a little tight. You think, *I might need these in case I go horseback riding one day.* You give the jeans away. Lo and behold, a friend asks you to go horseback riding a few weeks later. You think, "I should have kept those jeans!" Let me be honest with you. Even if the old jeans you gave away now seem perfect and you regret it, they weren't. They fit awkward and held the energy of the past. In fact, the opportunity to go horseback riding just may have presented itself as a result of clearing out the past.

Furthermore, wear your current jeans that you feel great in. Live in the moment, not the past. You will feel so much better and have a much better horseback-riding experience. Had you kept the old jeans and the experience had still presented itself, you wouldn't feel nearly as good as you would in the new jeans. Worst-case scenario: you have to buy new jeans. Not so bad.

But let me be really honest. It's not even about having to repurchase new jeans. It's not about the money. It's not about the inconvenience. It's about what those old jeans represented. What time in your life do they represent? There was some identity that you associated with those jeans for them to be up for debate at all. It may be as simple as you looked great in those jeans in 2008 when you were a size smaller. Maybe you had a great date in those jeans. Maybe someone complimented you when you wore them. Maybe you felt confident in those jeans. They represent positive memories, which is good, but it's still an old aspect that is stuck in the past, evidenced by them hanging on the rack unworn. I encourage feeling great in your current clothes, even if a size bigger. Embody your present self. You may already be doing this, but I encourage you to do so even more by releasing your past self.

The same principle applies whether it is clothing, kitchen utensils, or office supplies. Any time you hear yourself using the *just in case* excuse, investigate further. What does this item remind me of? What time period of my life is it from? What identity does this item represent? Whatever answer you come up with may seem trivial or insignificant, but it's not. These items represent the lingering thoughts and associations in the many crevices of our brain. By unlocking these memories, we can finally release and integrate the past.

I'll Get It Fixed

Once you've overcome the *just in case* excuse, don't let the *I'll get it fixed* excuse creep up on you. Lamps, dressers, chairs, curios, jewelry boxes, radios—the list goes on. These are just some of the many items I've heard people want to hang on to because they're "going to get it fixed." Other times, clients are conflicted about keeping a broken item when they know it can't be fixed but still love it. Fixable or not, these broken items spin us into confusion. There's no answer that feels right, so the item gets put back up for review at a later date, when hopefully the answer will magically come or the item will miraculously fix itself.

If you've kept a broken item for longer
than six months, then chances are really
high that you're not going to get it fixed.

If you've kept a broken item for longer than six months, then chances are really high that you're not going to get it fixed. Items that we truly value, whether sentimental or functional, we get fixed rather quickly. If you're using the *I'll get it fixed* excuse, then recognize that it's just that—an excuse for something else. The only question is, what's the real reason?

Cover excuses are always cover-ups for deep-rooted emotions and require more inquiry. Who gave it to you? Who does the item remind you of? Who or what story is connected to the item and is the reason you're keeping it? For example, maybe it's a jewelry box your grandmother gave you. If it were just any jewelry box, it would have been long gone. But the sentimentality is what's keeping your decision at bay.

In this case, it's important to fully flesh out the story around the item. This will give you clues to the energy around it. Are you keeping it because no one else in the family wanted it and so you feel like you should be the one to hold on to it? What was the energy around it being given to you? Are you holding the brokenness for that family line? What aspect of that relationship brings up the energy of brokenness or heartbreak?

There are never any accidents. Did the item break while in your possession? If so, under what circumstances did it break? Get to the bottom of the story around this item. Notice what emotions come up while exploring it. These emotions are why you've been holding on to the item. After that, whether you keep it or not will feel less weighted. By lifting the buried emotions, you will have more clarity about your next steps with the item. It's the stored emotions that cloud decision-making. When they're no longer at issue, the fog lifts and action can be taken.

For functional items with little or no meaning to them, your holding on may relate to the *just in case* excuse. Review the previous section for how your excuse may relate to lack. You might be keeping it just in case you decide to *get it fixed*. That's a real mind bender. If you grew up in a household where finances were strained, then perhaps there was a need to make use of any pieces and parts available. Ask yourself if the messaging you received in childhood about money still holds true for you or if it is contributing to your clutter and consequentially blocking your flow of abundance.

For My Kids

Your kids don't want your stuff either. This was the conclusion in a *Washington Post* article on March 27, 2015, by Jura Koncius, called "Stuff It: Millennials Nix Their Parents' Treasures." The article pointed out that as baby boomers lighten their load, they try to pawn their stuff off on their kids. But they don't want it either. This is consistent with what I've observed with clients. The once-coveted handmade bedroom suite passed down for generations finds itself on Craigslist instead. Regardless of our generation, we're all feeling the desire to live lighter.

The last several generations have evolved from savers to consumers to experiencers. The baby boomer generation is stuck between saving and consuming and now feels overloaded with stuff. Experiences and services are favored over physical objects (except for the phones, tablets, and computers that are needed to share the experiences). From a ten-second video to a 140-character entry, we share the evidence of our experience.

Because of the mass production of consumer items now, what was once a big deal to purchase is now something we don't think twice about. Not only that, but essential items are used as much for a sense of self-expression as they are for functionality. For example, a stainless-steel French press coffeemaker is not only an everyday functional item, but it's also an expression of the owner's personality, perhaps even showing up in their social media feed pictured with the perfect cup of coffee. With the change in consumerism, most people prefer picking out their own items instead of receiving the hand-me-down Mr. Coffee machine from Mom and Dad, let alone the overstuffed plaid armchair from 1988.

If you're keeping items for your kids, be realistic. If your kids are adults, then ask them if they want them. Unless they give you a definitive yes followed by them coming to get it, then this excuse is no longer valid. If they're not sure, then give them a certain time by which to make a decision. If they say no and you're still waffling, then you know it's a cover excuse for something else that relates back to your past that you're reluctant to let go of and you're using your kids as an excuse. If it's memorabilia items, refer to "Children's Memorabilia" in chapter 5.

The same applies if you're attempting to pass items off to other family members. It's an attempt to not feel emotion, namely guilt. Instead, you attempt to bypass the guilt of giving away items to others. If this is you, acknowledge the desire for fewer things or for items that are more in alignment with who you are today, not twenty years ago. This applies to taking on family items too. Don't become your ancestral family's dumping ground, unless it's with items you really want. Otherwise, you will be the holder of the family guilt.

It's Worth a Lot of Money

Other common excuses I hear from clients are *It's too good to just give it away*, *I paid a lot of money for that*, *It's worth a lot of money*, and *That seems like a waste.* First off, is it really worth a lot of money? We generally overvalue our stuff. This tends to be true with our home or car. Have you ever had a realtor or car salesman tell you the shockingly low comp value for your home or trade-in value for your car? Did you just about fall over in your chair like me? *There's no way that can be right. My home is worth more than that.* This is usually the case with our possessions in general. Sure, you may have paid eight hundred dollars for that couch, but it's only worth about eighty if you try to resell it.

For items that really are valuable, you may want to take the extra time to sell them. This is where time and money differ for each person. For one person, making extra cash on consignment clothes may be worth the extra time it takes rather than donating them. For someone else, it may feel like a waste of time. Selling items on Craigslist or eBay can be monetarily beneficial for some and a time waster for others. If an item holds significant value and is worth your time to sell, then decide your next course of action. If you don't want to take the time to sell it yourself, there are people and services that can do this for you. But make sure you're not using it as a stall tactic in disguise, as is often the case.

I recently had a client who was reluctant to give away a didgeridoo, a long wind instrument that's as challenging to play as it is to pronounce. She didn't want it anymore. Even though money wasn't an issue, she immediately said, "Well, that's too good to just give away." Really? I presented to her a story in which someone walks into a donation center, sees the didgeridoo, and is elated that they can finally buy one that is affordable.

I didn't push the issue, but most likely she paid quite a bit for the instrument and ended up using it very little. Getting some value back would relieve her guilt. Guilt is almost always the underlying emotion when it comes to an inner dialogue around money. I assure you though that storing guilt in your closet comes with a much higher price tag. As long as you're in vibrational alignment with guilt by keeping these guilt-filled items, you're more likely to accumulate more of them.

> We overestimate the worth of our items
> but underestimate the value in the
> experience of the purchase itself.

We overestimate the worth of our items but underestimate the value in the experience of the purchase itself. For purchases that are not necessities, much of the value is in the moment we purchase them, not too unlike buying an ice cream cone that we enjoy for the next ten minutes or making a ten-dollar roulette bet for the thrill of the moment. Be okay with that. Enjoy the moment. Someone else will enjoy attempting to play the didgeridoo too—for a moment.

I Don't Want to Add to Landfills

As more people are becoming sensitive to environmental issues, the excuse of not wanting to add to landfills is also becoming more common. Who can argue with being environmentally conscious, especially when it's a genuine concern? We often use the act of helping out others as an excuse for keeping stuff.

My kids may want my high school ring.

My sister may want this corduroy blazer with the arm patches.

We trick ourselves into believing we are helping others when it's really just our way of putting off making an honest decision about an item. The same thing happens with the *I don't want to add to landfills* excuse. You've gone from helping one person to saving the whole planet.

Let me be the one to burst your bubble: you're not doing the planet any favors by making your closet or garage or kitchen drawer its own landfill. What's the benefit of making your space a dump of useless items as opposed to a designated area where it can be appropriately compacted and take up much less space?

If you find you are using the landfill excuse, it's most likely a cover excuse for guilt. When we feel guilt, we generally overcompensate by trying to be "good." Saving the planet is a virtuous compensation for spending money on what turned out to be a seemingly wasteful item. Sure, we don't often make the best decisions in life. We do things we later regret, whether it's spending money or how we treated a friend or partner. But we live and learn. We forgive ourselves and others.

Give yourself a break if you bought an item that you never wore, never used, or simply paid too much for. Let it go. And by letting go of the item, you can let go of the guilt. Holding on to it and stuffing it in the back of your closet will only fester the emotion to the point where you have not only your own personal landfill but also a toxic dump.

If environmentalism is truly important to you, there are much better ways to direct your passions than creating your own closet dumpsite. Start with reducing consumption, which is the first step of the environmental slogan *reduce, reuse, recycle*. Here are some tips on being green while decluttering:

Reduce

The best thing about clearing clutter is that once it's gone, once you realize just how much you've accumulated, and once you realize how little you really need, then you are much less likely to consume as much in the future. Clearing clutter reduces future consumption. After clearing out your clutter, you will feel so much lighter that you will not want to reclutter your space. And when you do get the itch for something new, you will be much more choosey in what you purchase.

Clearing clutter
reduces future consumption.

Reuse

The second-best way to be green is to reuse. One of the best ways to reuse items is to donate them to organizations where they can be used again. Keep a giveaway bag for periodically collecting items for giving away. Make sure these items are reusable and not items that should be recycled or thrown away. For example, your favorite sneakers from 1988 that have holes and worn-out soles probably shouldn't be reused.

More websites and mobile apps are being created to make reusing items more available and efficient. Craigslist and eBay are the most common sites, but more companies are making selling and buying consignment goods incredibly easy through your smartphone. If your time is more important, then consider donating your items to organizations in need of household goods and clothing. Refer to the appendix of this book for a list of resources to make reusing easy and even profitable.

Recycle

Now that you have pared down your items to those no longer reusable, it's time to recycle. If you don't already recycle paper, glass, aluminum, and plastic on a regular basis, then start now. Every major city has recycling centers, if they don't already pick up at your home. For items that you're uncertain about, check out Earth911.org. It's a great resource for finding what you can recycle based upon your zip code, from mattresses to computer monitors to eyeglasses.

For items that you want to get rid of but are not reusable or recyclable, head to the dump. You may have a genuine concern about contributing to the earth's landfills, but it will give you new insight into future purchases as you consider whether an item is a win-win for you and the planet.

It's All My Spouse's Stuff

When I facilitate workshops or book events, regardless of the topic, it's only a matter of time until a participant brings up their spouse's stuff as the source of their clutter issues. This is another attempt at pointing the finger outward instead of inward. Relationships are our best mirrors, so it makes sense that we would look to our partner as the source of our clutter problems.

This excuse comes predominantly from women blaming their husbands for household clutter issues, but it can certainly go in the opposite direction too. As I discussed in the previous chapter, men tend to resist their clutter issues more than women. Based on that observation, I have no doubt that there's some legitimacy to the women's question and concerns. But I find it's usually only half the story.

It's quite common for opposites to attract when it comes to clutter. The neat freak marries the packrat. It is nature's way of striving for balance. How each person in the relationship keeps a home can differ dramatically. These differences are a mirror for the differences of each person in the relationship. Our home is not only a mirror for ourselves but also the relationships taking place under the roof.

The best approach is to be the example for decluttering. Tend to your own clutter issues. Yours may just be more hidden than your partner's. Each time you are bothered by your partner's clutter, look at your own pile and see what you can let go of. Realize that blaming your spouse is just an excuse for your own resistance of letting go, perhaps not with clutter, but on an emotional or mental level instead.

CHAPTER 9

The Digital Clutter Crisis
Out of Sight, Out of Mind?

Taking control of our possessions in the physical world is quite a task. But it's nothing compared to the mass of information that we've been storing and will continue to store in the nontangible world. You've most likely already experienced a sampling of what the next generational clutter challenge will be: digital clutter. As we head further into the age of information and technology, all the data we are storing will be ground zero for the next clutter epidemic. Unlike our homes and closets, there is infinite space available in the cloud and therefore even more places to store and hide our stuff.

Clutter will be moving from the physical third dimension to the mental fourth dimension. I refer to the third dimension as the space where we can touch, taste, and smell physical items. The fourth dimension is the space in which our thoughts reside. Like an electronic file in the cloud, it's there even if you can't see it.

With each generation, technology becomes more integral to our everyday existence. Children intuitively know how to use computers and phones, whereas technology is a foreign language to older generations. Computer games and phone apps are replacing toys. I remember having a set of Sesame Street 45 records. That music would now be listened to as digital downloads on a mobile device.

We have more information floating around us than ever before. Information is energy. Instead of manila file folders in a filing cabinet, we can store the same information in a digital file folder on a computer and on a smart phone. Any information we need—photos, addresses, phone numbers, tax returns, money, and virtually any piece of information you can think of—is at our fingertips. The Digital Age has even turned physical objects into nonphysical objects. My iPhone can morph into an alarm clock, a Zen garden, a newspaper, a camera, a voice recorder, a board game, a flashlight, and much more. Before long, it might just become my nightstand.

Just like physical clutter, digital clutter
takes up valuable space and prevents
new things from coming in.

More digital storage has allowed us to free up our physical spaces, but we still have to be mindful of the energy that floats around us. We may have fewer physical objects around us, but we are overwhelmed with information more than ever. We must be conscious of what *information energy* we have hanging around us that might in fact be clutter. Just like physical clutter, digital clutter takes up valuable space and prevents new things from coming in. The amount of information we are able to process is limited. Don't clog up your valuable space. Know what's taking up your mental space and when your mental disk drive is full.

Moving from the physical dimension into the digital dimension is potentially good news for our physical spaces. You probably use and store much less paper than before. And honestly, there's little excuse now to have an overabundance of paper and files in your office space. Storing documents digitally will lighten up your workspace dramatically.

There is plenty of scientific research that now proves that a visually cluttered space leads to a cluttered mind. For this reason, storing data in the digital cloud is a great solution to streamlining our spaces. That being said, out of sight is not completely out of mind. Just because you can't see it doesn't mean it's not still cluttered. As the garbage dumps fill up, so does the cloud. Even though having fewer items sitting around cuts down on visual clutter, do you still feel like you're running from your stuff with nowhere to hide? The only difference is that it's now password protected.

Tips for Digital Decluttering

Our minds continue to expand and have the ability to hold more information, but there comes a time when enough is enough. These invisible storage areas can hide old emotions we haven't processed, just like our closets and physical storage spaces. We've just become more sophisticated in how we hide our past. The items from our past relationships, careers, and identities discussed in the previous chapters may be cleverly hiding in a computer file, in a Dropbox, or even with an online photo company. The following are just a few of the many places in your digital world you can start decluttering.

These invisible storage areas can hide old
emotions we haven't processed, just like
our closets and physical storage spaces.
We've just become more sophisticated
in how we hide our past.

Phone Contacts

When was the last time you updated your phone contacts? Chances are there are people in your contacts that you no longer socialize with, do business with, or even want contact with at all. Clear them out. Although your phone may be able to hold a thousand more contacts, you still need to *make space* for new people to come into your life. This is a great way to allow space for new people to come into your life—for business, friendship, or romance.

Computer File Folders

If your computer file folders were in a filing cabinet, would they be bulging over? Most likely, yes. My favorite time to clean up my computer files is when I'm traveling on an airplane. Too cheap to pay the extra Wi-Fi charge, I start organizing and deleting files on my computer. If you haven't already, take the time to organize your computer files into folders and subfolders. Move files into their appropriate folder and then delete the ones you no longer need. Like your desk, the more organized your computer files, the clearer you will be able to think.

Also take the time to back up your important documents. Store any documents that you would be lost without if your computer crashed on a zip drive. For smaller documents, you can email them to yourself or upload to Google Drive, Dropbox, or some other online storage destination so they are stored somewhere else besides your hard drive.

Online Storage

Storing information in online storage sites is similar to renting a storage bin. We have so much stuff that it won't all fit in our space. Online storage options provided by Apple, Google, and many other companies allow for our digital minds to continue expanding. It seems like with each new phone I buy, I have to upgrade the storage because of the expansion of information I process in just a couple of years.

Online storage is also handy for storing important duplicates to share with others or as a backup in case of a hard drive crash or other calamity. But, again, be mindful of the information you are storing. The next time you are alerted that you've reached your storage capacity, see if there are some old files you can delete. The past may be present in your online storage just like it is in your off-site storage.

Emails

Does your email inbox stack up like the snail mail on your kitchen counter? We get inundated with a barrage of emails daily. If you aren't proactive, it can overtake you within a few days. Implement a system for organizing your emails. Like with physical mail, immediately throw away or delete junk mail. This will easily eliminate 90 percent of your emails. For the emails you may want to look at later, set up a *read later* folder in your email account. For emails with important information, save in a *keep* folder. Your inbox should then only have the emails that require your immediate attention.

Photos

Staying on top of photos has never been more challenging. Between our phones, tablets, computers, and online photo companies, our digital photos are floating around everywhere. Whether stored in a computer file, a scrapbook, or your closet, photos hold energy. Everything discussed about photos thus far equally applies when they are in a digital format. Take inventory of what memories you're holding on to.

In the same way you organize computer files on your computer, do the same with your photos. Organize them by certain events or time periods in file folders. You can imagine each file folder as its own photo album. Back up important photos. Upload photos to an online photo company so that they can actually be printed if you decide you want a hard copy or even a whole photo album.

Social Media Sites

Once you post something on a social media site, such as Instagram, Facebook, or Twitter, you might think it will go down in history forever. But don't hesitate to go back and delete old entries or photos that don't resonate with you anymore. Your online accounts are your digital real estate. Keep them updated, especially if used for professional purposes. It may be fun to use old posts and photos for remembering the good times. But if there are photos or other memories that you don't want to be reminded of, then take ownership of your accounts and delete photos of not-so-good memories.

Desktop Icons and Phone Apps

Is your computer desktop full of files that you haven't properly filed away? What about software icons that you never use? These can cause some serious visual clutter that can lead to a cluttered mind. Peruse your desktop to see if there are items you can remove. The same is true with your phone. Are there apps on your various screens that you never use? Periodically, go through your phone apps and delete the ones that didn't live up to their hype or that you've lost interest in. It will just highlight the ones that you do use and love.

Bookmarks

Have your Internet bookmarks become so cluttered it's like surfing the web just to find the one you're looking for? Go through your bookmarks and delete the ones that no longer interest you. For bookmarks you want to keep but don't use that often, categorize them into bookmark folders, such as *recipes*, *travel*, and *good ideas*. Different browsers offer different methods of organizing bookmarks. Take advantage of these features.

Any technological organization is tedious but will save you time in the long run. Technology is meant to bring more ease and convey information at a faster pace. If it's slowing you down instead, then you know it's time to do some digital decluttering and organizing. Just like physical clutter, digital clutter not only slows us down from moving forward, but it also hides the good stuff—the stuff we really love and use.

Experiences Are the New Commodity

As a culture, we are trending toward minimalism and a "less is more" mentality. Perhaps this is balancing out the deluge of physical items piled up since the mass production of consumer goods that began in the 1950s. Younger generations are more mobile than ever before with the advent of our mobile technology age. Experiences are the new commodity.

Experiences may come in the form of services, travel, adventure, collaboration, and creative arts such as music, art, and writing. These may result in a tangible item, but in a lighter form than previous creations. For example, instead of a record album, it's a digital download or momentary streaming experience. Experiences are socially shareable, and that's what takes precedence.

Our current challenges with physical clutter will eventually fade once generation X and the millennials have sifted through what was left from the baby boomer generation. The baby boomer generation was a perfect storm for accumulating clutter. Following World War II, there was a suburban explosion of homes and furnishings being mass produced.

Between 1945 and 1960, the gross national product more than doubled. The middle class had more money to spend than ever before with more variety and availability of consumer goods. Add the fact that many baby boomers grew up following the Depression era—a time when possessions represented survival for many middle-class households. You can see how consuming and holding on to things became a way of life.

Digital clutter will be our next battle. The nonphysical space of the Internet, including the cloud, is basically the mind of the collective consciousness that has the potential to expand infinitely. Tangible objects will continue to hold interest. Holding, feeling, and touching an actual book will remain more satisfying than a digital book can ever be. And yet the convenience of a digital book can't be replaced by lugging a hardback around. Both physical and digital platforms of consumer goods have appeal in different ways.

In the current social media era, experiences and moments rule the day. If what we value most is a quick pic of me and my friends at the pool that was shared on Snapchat and disappeared within twenty-four hours, are we at risk of losing our past? Will we have any record of our heritage? What about the recipe cards that were once filed in a recipe box and passed on to generations? Will we instead give a URL to our food board on Pinterest? Will we be scrolling through our Instagram account with our grandkids? Are we putting our history in the hands of social media companies that could disappear tomorrow? But then again, do we really need a past?

Losing the Past to the Present

More photos have been taken in the last five years than in our entire history combined. It's estimated that 99 percent of those photos will never be printed. Will we have anything to show for our life? Is it possible that we're actually spending more time in the present moment than reminiscing about the past?

Living in the present moment has been a virtue sought after for thousands of years in spirituality. In Buddhist philosophy, the impermanence of life and the importance of living fully in each moment is a primary principle. One ritual that Tibetan Buddhist monks participate in is the creation of an intricate sand mandala over several days or even weeks just to brush it away at the end in a demonstration of the transitory nature of life. Are today's social media entries any different?

When I see my teenage niece interacting with her friends on Snapchat, I wonder if what seems like attention-deficit behavior to adults is actually a series of living-in-the-moment moments. Will younger generations one day regret not saving more photos? Maybe. Not taking the oak dining room set? Doubtful. Not saving family photos? Probably. When you're young, you don't think you'll ever be old or that loved ones will depart. As we get older, we collect more moments to cherish, but also more moments to release.

Is It Okay to Get Rid of Memorabilia?

In our culture, nostalgia is generally considered a good thing. We've been programmed to believe we need to keep memorabilia. But is this true? It really comes down to whether an item from the past is providing good memories or positive energy from which to springboard, or if it is festering bad memories or negative patterns. A picture is worth a thousand words, but are they good words? Most memorabilia fall in between these two extremes, making it difficult to decide whether it's worth keeping or not.

Keeping too much memorabilia can also
physically and energetically weigh
us down and trap us in a hamster wheel
of re-creating the past.

Memorabilia can be grounding. They can transport us back to special times. We can see how far we've come. Keeping too much memorabilia can also physically and energetically weigh us down and trap us in a hamster wheel of re-creating the past. Too much memorabilia can potentially keep you locked in the past and prevent you from moving forward or from being present in your current life.

A balance between the past and the future is the key. If you find it challenging to move forward in your life, get past certain events from your past, or feel stuck, then cleaning out memorabilia can possibly set you free. How do you know what the right amount is for you? Think about how much space you want memorabilia take up. Is it an entire room, an entire closet, a storage container, a shoebox, a jump drive? I have one storage container that is about three-quarters full. I call it my memory box. If it starts to get so full that I can't close the lid, then it's time to remove one or more items. One generous-sized box of the past is plenty for me. I tend to remember too much of the past as it is.

Memorabilia are memory keepers and hold powerful energy. Just revisiting memorabilia will stir energy and emotions. One client told me that as she was clearing out college memorabilia, she came across a T-shirt from an old boyfriend. Within hours, he contacted her out of the blue. Items hold memories, which are simply stored energy. Once she activated the energy, her thoughts put into motion an event to bring resolution to that relationship that was otherwise stored away in her subconscious mind. This is why clearing out these items can be a powerful modality for healing.

Consider releasing anything that conjures up negative feelings or memories. This stuck energy has been preventing you from moving forward in your life. Be conscious and present with what an item brings up for you. If you are not ready or it doesn't feel right, that's okay too. Many people don't get rid of memorabilia simply because they're not sure how. It doesn't feel right to just throw certain memories in the trash with last night's spaghetti. Maybe it feels wasteful to throw out a leather-bound journal. Or perhaps there's a fear of your privacy being violated.

For items of a sensitive nature, it might feel appropriate to dispose of them with a ceremony. The element of fire is commonly used to represent transformation. Releasing something into water can be cleansing. Burying an old letter into the earth can be healing. Give your process the due respect that it needs. Most importantly, be compassionate with yourself. And, as always, send items off with the farewell blessing: thank you and goodbye.

Clutter Clearing
Step-by-Step
Roll Up Your Sleeves

My hope is that by now you are motivated to roll up your sleeves and clear some clutter. With a new understanding of how your stuff is keeping you stuck, you have everything you need to now take action. If you need some practical elbow grease to get moving, then keep reading. This chapter will provide a step-by-step guide to decluttering.

You may not realize an item has an emotional charge until you begin sifting and sorting items into their goodbye bags and boxes. You may not have expected measuring spoons to bring up the past. Or maybe you forgot you still had photos of that certain someone. It's at this point that you might run into some resistance. Don't abandon ship. Don't shut down. You may need to refer to previous chapters to see what the trigger is.

If you find yourself having a lengthy dialogue with yourself about an item, then that's a red flag of an emotional component at play. Decision-making comes easy when an item has a neutral charge. If you find yourself stuck at any point, then it's most likely because unresolved emotions have gotten involved. See this as a good thing. You can now face the past and be done with it.

The number-one problem I hear from clients is that they are overwhelmed with their home and their clutter. This is reflective of feeling overwhelmed in life too. One's home will always reflect one's inner state of being, and vice versa. Tackling the home clutter will help you gain a sense of control over other areas of your life. As you declutter your home, you will also relieve feeling overwhelmed in other areas of your life. But most people don't know where to begin.

Starting a decluttering project is similar to staring a weight loss program. It feels like a daunting feat to lose a hundred pounds, or even twenty. You want a magic wand to make it immediately go away. But to make significant change, we have to shift internally on the emotional level, as discussed thus far, but also on the physical level through action steps. Now it's time to take the action steps of decluttering.

Keep in mind, however, that attempting to take action is futile if there's shame around the situation. This is why someone who loses weight may immediately gain it back, in addition to tacking on some extra pounds. The root cause hasn't been addressed. The same is true with clearing clutter. If the underlying cause hasn't been uncovered, then you will only clear out to acquire more later on.

It may be helpful to work with a coach, therapist, mentor, energy healer, or conscious community in tandem with major purging projects. Remember that having too much stuff is simply the symptom, not the problem. Clutter is distraction from what we don't want to face in our life. The good news is that once you have awareness of the underlying issue, you can take action rather quickly. The following sections will guide you from start to finish on decluttering your home with ease and grace.

Create One Area You Love

If you know your decluttering project is going to take place over many weeks or months, I recommend creating one area in your home that you absolutely love. Make this your refuge. This could be your bathtub, meditation space, reading nook, kitchen, or bedroom. Like a meditation, this is the space you can always retreat when everything else seems chaotic. This will also provide you with inspiration for other areas of your home.

Ask for Help

Sometimes we just need help. It's hard to see the forest for the trees when it comes to our home. We're simply too close to it and can't always see our blind spots. Hiring someone with an objective pair of eyes, such as a professional organizer or feng shui consultant, can lighten your load and help you get the perspective you need. Or grab a friend who will be honest with you. Who knows? She may want the one thing you need to get rid of.

Remove Easy Things First

The first step to decluttering is to start in easy areas first. Start with the nonemotional, nontriggering, easy-breezy stuff first, not the gut-wrenching, Kleenex-box-grabbing items that you could mull and cry over for a week. Move out as much stuff in the shortest amount of time possible just to get the energy moving. Think of this as the expired food in the fridge. No matter how desperate you get, you know you're not going to eat it. There's no decision to make.

These items can be anything from papers to furniture. Yes, furniture. Unused, ill-placed, nonfunctional furniture can be one of the biggest clutter items. Move it out. Create space. The more space you can immediately free up, the sooner you can get the ball rolling. Space gives us energy. It also gives us clarity. As the fog slowly begins to lift, you will gain momentum and be energized to keep moving.

When I work with clients, it's not uncommon for them to start walking around the house grabbing lamps off tables and random decor items off shelves. They realize they don't like these items and haven't liked them for years. In other words, you can approach this step in an organized fashion or more organically by walking around the house randomly removing items. Again, the goal is to get energy moving—in you and your home.

This step should be enjoyable and freeing. It's like cutting junk food out of your diet that you never really liked but ate out of habit. Speaking of enjoyable, decluttering doesn't have to feel like a chore. Turn some music on, listen to an inspiring podcast, or add anything else that will make it a positive experience. Let me give you permission to go ahead and take the day off work to declutter. After all, this is the best preventative medicine there is.

Make a List

Once the easy stuff is out of the way, it's time to prioritize the other areas in your home. Simply make a list of the areas you want to declutter. You'd be amazed at what simple pen and paper can do to relieve feeling overwhelmed. This is when our logical, analytical brain can step in and help out immensely.

Simply write a to-do list. Getting things on paper will get it out of your head and give you relief. Don't worry about tackling the list just yet. You're simply looking for a better feeling than overwhelmed. Once you have your list, then you can once again start with the easier areas first.

If it took one year or twenty years to create a basement full of clutter, don't expect to clear it out in an hour. Set realistic goals. For example, if you're taking on a monumental task such as cleaning out the basement, then break it down into smaller steps. If you're cleaning out a closet, focus on one section at a time. It's easy to get stopped in our tracks by something that seems too big to accomplish. We end up abandoning it before we ever get started. Breaking it down into bite-sized steps will give the space you need to get moving. For example, if you want to declutter your kitchen and pantry, make a detailed list. It might start out like this:

KITCHEN
- Refrigerator
    > Clean out expired and uneaten foods
    > Wipe down shelves
- Repeat with freezer

Continue with each area of the kitchen. Take one step at a time and don't rush the process. You will feel a sense of accomplishment as you make your way down the list and cross each task off. If helpful, reward yourself upon each accomplishment. However, you will find that the best reward will inherently be the renewed feeling of the cleared space.

Be Present

Decluttering can be a meditative process. You may be surprised at what messages come through or what emotions or memories come up. Objects have a field, just as humans do, that carries energy and associated memories. If an object stirs emotions in you, don't ignore them. Instead, explore them and feel them. This will facilitate the process of releasing the item. Once you're finished, be present and notice how you feel. Most likely you'll feel much lighter.

One way to become more present is to hold an intention of what you want to accomplish. Your intention may be to make your bedroom cozier, to create more space in your closet for new clothes, or to attract a new relationship. Your intention can be as general or specific as you want it to be. Knowing what you want as a result will give you more incentive to plow forward.

Set Aside Time

Dealing with areas in your home or office that have piled up for years most likely calls for a more scheduled approach. Just like you would schedule time to meet with a client, you need to schedule time to declutter. It must be a priority or else it won't happen. You take time out to accumulate things, so take time to release things too. Create a block of time out of your schedule. Take a day off from work or carve out an afternoon or simply designate the next thirty minutes for clearing clutter.

As we become energetically lighter,
certain items from the past
are no longer a vibrational match.

Sometimes you might have a sudden urge to purge. When these times come up, go with it. I find that this is when I'm most productive because I have an inner urge to let items go. Clearing clutter can be an instinctive process, just like a mother "nesting" prior to giving birth. It's also common to purge after experiencing a spiritual awakening or milestones along your path of self-growth. As we become energetically lighter, certain items from the past are no longer a vibrational match. It is a natural process, like a snake shedding its skin or even the digestive system eliminating waste.

Divide and Conquer

Decluttering requires some supplies. Make sure you have boxes, bags, and a recycling bin on hand. Permanent markers are great for labeling boxes. This step is important because you don't want to clear one closet just to shift it all into another one. While you are clearing, you want to be able to immediately place the item into its destination to reduce any further clutter. As you start the clearing process, it is help-ful to sort the items into the following piles or sections:

- Trash
- Recycling
- Returns
- Donation
- For sale
- Undecided

Place trash items in trash bags. Place recyclable items in a recy-cling container immediately. Place returns in a designated box. Place items that will be donated in an appropriate bag or box for immedi-ate delivery. Make sure items you have designated to sell are worth your time to sell and that you're not using the "for sale" items as a way to distract yourself into keeping them. Also refer to the clutter clearing flowchart in the appendix when you start sifting and sorting.

Designate one pile of stuff as "undecided." Deal with these items last. The reason for this is you don't want those items to keep you from moving out the easy stuff. Have you ever started decluttering and you come across a magazine or some other resource and find yourself rereading the entire magazine? Before you know it, half an hour has passed. Avoid this. Instead put it in a pile for later. Better yet, tear the article out or toss the magazine out altogether. If you haven't taken action on it yet, you probably never will.

Decide on Undecided Items

Deciding on undecided items is the quintessential question of clear-ing clutter and the central focus of this book. As a reminder, clutter is anything that keeps you in the past and prevents you from living the life you want to be living. It's no longer serving your highest and best inter-est. This is regardless of monetary value. A two-hundred-dollar Water-ford crystal can be clutter if it was a gift that you don't particularly like but feel guilty getting rid of. On the other hand, a piece of scrap paper with an inspiring quote might not be clutter if it's still providing value to you.

Clearing clutter is a very subjective process that ironically requires a great deal of objectivity. In determining what to keep, first consider:

• Do I use it?

• Do I love it?

Professional organizer and author Marie Kondo suggests asking yourself, "Does it spark joy?" You should love or lovingly use everything in your home. If you don't, then it's taking up valuable space. If you're still struggling with an item, then it most likely falls within one of the categories in the preceding chapters. This is when more self-inquiry is necessary. Start asking yourself these questions:

• What am I feeling right now?

• What memories does this item bring up?

• Who gave it to me?

• Why did I originally buy it?

• Who does it remind me of?

• Do I feel guilty getting rid of this item? If so, why?

• What time of my life was I in when I used this?

Get to the root of why you are hanging on to an item that you know is no longer serving you. What you thought was just an old mug may actually be a reservoir of past emotions that you and your past love shared on a trip to San Francisco. Or maybe the green strapless dress with the price tag on it conjures up guilt for buying things that are on sale and never wearing them. Until acknowledged, the energy behind these items will continue in your energy field like a live wire.

After further inquiry, if you're still unsure about an item, that's okay too. It will come back around for review in the next round of decluttering. By then, you might have new insight or be in a place of letting it go. Sometimes we simply need more time before letting something go that was emotionally sensitive. Like everything in life, we hold on to it until becomes easier not to.

One approach is to pack undecided items in a box and store them. Within a year, revisit the items and see if you're still undecided. Most likely you won't be. You'll wonder why you felt a need to hang on to them and most likely forgot you even had them. Each time you clear clutter you will be amazed at how much easier it gets. It becomes extremely freeing. When you successfully do it once, you realize life really does continue without those items.

The Body Knows Best

When all else fails in deciding whether to keep an item, turn to your body. The mental mind can have us going back and forth like we're watching a tennis match. Even after reading up to this point, you may still be deluding yourself, or not trusting yourself, about a certain item. Your body never lies, though. Your body is intricately connected to your subconscious and will tell you the truth. It's an extremely useful tool in discerning whether you should hang on to an item or not.

Marie Kondo's test is helpful because of its simplicity. Also, the phrase "spark joy" speaks more to our emotional body than our mental body. And yet if we toss this question around for too long, we can start to lose the feeling state and go into our head. Even if an item doesn't spark joy, you may still be reluctant to get rid of it because of the stored emotions around the item that need to be released. Consult your body for the real truth.

There are several ways to use the body as a truth-telling device. I once had the opportunity to have a friend who is a practicing kinesiologist over to my home. Applied kinesiology is a technique used to tap into the subconscious mind through our muscles. It's often referred to as *muscle testing* and is most commonly performed by holding out your arm in tandem with the applied kinesiologist asking certain questions. For a negative answer, the arm will go weak. For a positive answer, the arm will remain strong.

My friend muscle-tested me about random household items I had lying around. I was shocked at my body's responses. For example, there were some trendy pillows that I thought I should like, but my body didn't agree. I share this as an example of how the body knows best. If you have the opportunity to work with applied kinesiology, try using it with items about which you're unsure. You might be surprised to find that you don't like that piece of artwork in your foyer after all.

A technique that you can use anytime and anywhere is using your body as a compass. This technique can be used for any decision-making situations. Hold the item in your hand. Or set it on a table. If it's a large item, then stand close to it. Close your eyes or gently gaze at the item. Quiet your mind, breathe, and direct all your focus to your body.

Feel into your body and notice if your body tends to sway toward the item or away from it. Notice any other sensations in the body. This will give you your answer whether to keep the item or not. If your body leans toward the item, then it's a keeper. If your body moves away from the item, then it's time for it to go.

If you question your body or don't get a clear yes or no, then there may be more to uncover. The item might hold contradictory feelings for you. If this is the case, then ask yourself some questions:

• What feelings does it bring up?
• Who does it remind me of?

- Who gave it to me?
- What emotions do I feel holding this item?

You can continue using the body as a compass for more answers.

For items with mixed messages, don't feel pressured into letting go of it just because you think you should. Take some time to reveal to yourself what's really at the root of it. You can then say thank you and goodbye with confidence. The more you start feeling into your body, the more you will tune in to its messages. If you're clearing out items and suddenly feel sick to your stomach or inordinately tired, then there is a strong negative emotion around an item or items.

It's important to drink plenty of water
and be mindful of your energy level
when decluttering.

It's important to drink plenty of water and be mindful of your energy level when decluttering. You are shifting a lot of energy. Even the most benign objects hold energy of some sort. And while letting items go will ultimately lift you energetically, the emotion-filled items will likely stir emotions within you that need your attention. This is serious energy work, similar to receiving a massage, bodywork, or energy healing. Notice if certain items suddenly cause a change in you physically. This is a red flag that there is more to this item than you realize.

It's also not uncommon for sensitive people to experience physical ailments as a result of decluttering. You may be surprised by the amount of energy you are shifting when decluttering. If you or others in your household start feeling sick with a cold, allergies, stomach illness, or other ailments, then it might be wise to slow down the decluttering process. You may need time to integrate the changes that you have made. When you are feeling healthy again, dive back in.

Final Step: Delivery

The final step is to actually get the items out of your house. Until this happens, you're not done. It's best to arrange this step sooner than later so that it doesn't become a stall tactic. Depending on the size of your load, you may need to enlist help with this step. If it's a manageable load, then transfer it to your car as soon as possible. It's that much closer to its destination. If it's too much to handle, then arrange an organization to pick it up at your home for donation. If the items are beyond use, then consider hiring a company that specializes in transporting junk. See the appendix for a list of organizations and companies that can assist in this process.

Conclusion

You've made it this far and have everything you need to start your clutter intervention. You now realize that decluttering is more of an inside job than manual labor. Once you jump through the emotional and mental hurdles of why you've been holding on to your stuff, the actual decluttering is easy and liberating. Now that you can see how your stuff has been keeping you stuck in the past, it's time to get started.

During the process, be objective while being present and compassionate for yourself. Think of yourself as your two-year-old self with your first toy. Letting go is not any easier now than it was then. And yet, you now have the understanding and desire to step forward into a life that represents your authentic self.

My wish is that you continue to evolve and expand into the future with ease and grace, while enjoying those items that enhance the best aspects of you and bring you the most joy.

Appendix

Websites and Mobile Apps for Consignment Goods

Craigslist.com

eBay.com

LetGo.com

Listia.com

Mercari.com

Poshmark.com

Thredup.com

Tradesy.com

Vinted.com

Charitable Organizations for Donating Goods

Big Brother Big Sister Foundation—Bbbsfoundation.org

Brides Across America—Bridesacrossamerica.com

Dress For Success—Dressforsuccess.org

Goodwill—Goodwill.org

The Salvation Army—Salvationarmy.org

Soles4Souls—Soles4souls.org

Vietnam Veterans of America—Pickupplease.org

Clutter Clearing Flowchart

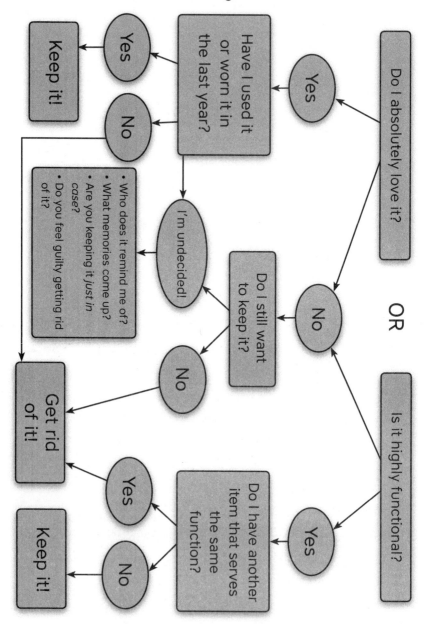

Bibliography

Campbell, Joseph. *The Hero with a Thousand Faces*. New York: Pantheon, 1949.

Chapman, Gary. *The 5 Love Languages: The Secret to Love That Lasts*. Chicago: Northfield Publishing, 2009.

Chauran, Alexandra. *Clearing Clutter: Physical, Mental, and Spiritual*. Woodbury, MN: Llewellyn Publishing, 2015.

Chopra, Deepak, Debbie Ford, and Marianne Williamson. *The Shadow Effect: Illuminating the Hidden Power of Your True Self*. New York: Harper Collins, 2010.

Ford, Debbie. *The Dark Side of the Light Chasers: Reclaiming Your Power, Creativity, Brilliance, and Dreams*. New York: Riverhead Books, 2010.

Jung, Carl. *Memories, Dreams, Reflections*. New York: Vintage, 1965.

———. *Psychology and Alchemy*. Vol. 12, *The Collected Works of C. G. Jung*. Princeton, NJ: Princeton University Press, 1968.

Kondo, Marie. *The Life-Changing Magic of Tidying Up*. Berkeley, CA: Ten Speed Press, 2014.

Kübler-Ross, Elisabeth, and David Kessler. *On Grief and Grieving: Finding the Meaning of Grief Through the Five Stages of Loss.* New York: Scribner, 2005.

Moore, Thomas. *Dark Nights of the Soul: A Guide to Finding Your Way Through Life's Ordeals.* New York: Gotham Books, 2004.

Nhat Hanh, Thich. *Fragrant Palm Leaves: Journals, 1962–1966.* New York: Riverhead Trade, 1999.

Richo, David. *The Five Things We Cannot Change: And the Happiness We Find by Embracing Them.* Boston: Shambhala, 2016.

———. *When the Past Is Present: Healing the Emotional Wounds That Sabotage Our Relationships.* Boston: Shambhala, 2008.

Swan, Teal. *The Completion Process: The Practice of Putting Yourself Back Together Again.* Carlsbad, CA: Hay House, 2016.

Tharp, Twyla. *The Creative Habit: Learn It and Use It For Life.* New York: Simon & Schuster, 2009.

Weil, Sharon. *ChangeAbility: How Artists, Activists, and Awakeners Navigate Change.* Los Angeles: Archer, 2016.

Wolynn, Mark. *It Didn't Start with You: How Inherited Family Trauma Shapes Who We Are and How to End the Cycle.* New York: Viking, 2016.

To Write to the Author

If you wish to contact the author or would like more information about this book, please write to the author in care of Llewellyn Worldwide Ltd. and we will forward your request. Both the author and publisher appreciate hearing from you and learning of your enjoyment of this book and how it has helped you. Llewellyn Worldwide Ltd. cannot guarantee that every letter written to the author can be answered, but all will be forwarded. Please write to:

Tisha Morris
℅ Llewellyn Worldwide
2143 Wooddale Drive
Woodbury, MN 55125-2989

Please enclose a self-addressed stamped envelope for reply,
or $1.00 to cover costs. If outside the U.S.A., enclose
an international postal reply coupon.

Many of Llewellyn's authors have websites with additional information and resources. For more information, please visit our website at http://www.llewellyn.com.

GET MORE AT LLEWELLYN.COM

Visit us online to browse hundreds of our books and decks, plus sign up to receive our e-newsletters and exclusive online offers.

- Free tarot readings • Spell-a-Day • Moon phases
- Recipes, spells, and tips • Blogs • Encyclopedia
- Author interviews, articles, and upcoming events

GET SOCIAL WITH LLEWELLYN

Find us on f
www.Facebook.com/LlewellynBooks

🐦 @LlewellynBooks

GET BOOKS AT LLEWELLYN

LLEWELLYN ORDERING INFORMATION

Order online: Visit our website at www.llewellyn.com to select your books and place an order on our secure server.

Order by phone:
- Call toll free within the U.S. at 1-877-NEW-WRLD (1-877-639-9753)
- Call toll free within Canada at 1-866-NEW-WRLD (1-866-639-9753)
- We accept VISA, MasterCard, American Express and Discover

Order by mail:
Send the full price of your order (MN residents add 6.875% sales tax) in U.S. funds, plus postage and handling to: Llewellyn Worldwide, 2143 Wooddale Drive Woodbury, MN 55125-2989

POSTAGE AND HANDLING

STANDARD (U.S. & Canada):
(Please allow 12 business days)
$30.00 and under, add $4.00.
$30.01 and over, FREE SHIPPING.

INTERNATIONAL ORDERS:
$16.00 for one book, plus $3.00 for each additional book.

Visit us online for more shipping options. Prices subject to change.

FREE CATALOG!

To order, call
1-877-NEW-WRLD
ext. 8236
or visit our
website

Transform Your Life One Room at a Time

MIND
BODY
HOME

TISHA MORRIS

Mind, Body, Home
Transform Your Life One Room at a Time
TISHA MORRIS

Awaken to the energetic connections between you and your home. When you make conscious changes to your living space, you can transform your life and uncover your soul.

Unlike other books of its kind, *Mind, Body, Home* presents your home as an integral component to holistic living. From foundation to roof, this essential guide correlates every component of your house with its physical, mental, or emotional counterpart in you. Your home becomes a reflection of you, and being more in tune with your home's energy will allow you to make positive changes in your life. Open the door to the heart of your home and discover a whole new way of seeing and living within it!

978-0-7387-3694-5, 264 pp., 6 x 9   **$16.99**

DECORATING

WITH THE

FIVE ELEMENTS

OF

FENG SHUI

Tisha Morris

Author of *Mind, Body, Home*

Decorating With the
Five Elements of Feng Shui
TISHA MORRIS

Balance your energy, improve your relationships and happiness, and heal your living space and the planet. Join feng shui expert Tisha Morris as she reveals the amazing possibilities for transformation when you use five elements wisdom to make simple yet beautiful changes in your home and life.

The five elements—Wood, Fire, Earth, Metal, Water—are the threads of energy that connect all living beings with nature. Learn how each element is expressed not only in nature, but also through you and your home. Start with a quiz to understand your elemental makeup. Then follow the three-step formula to incorporate feng shui into your life. With a room-to-room guide for using the five elements, instructions for healing spaces both inside and outside, and much more, *Decorating With the Five Elements of Feng Shui* will help you find harmony in your body, your home, and the world.

978-0-7387-4652-4, 264 pp., 6 x 9   **$16.99**

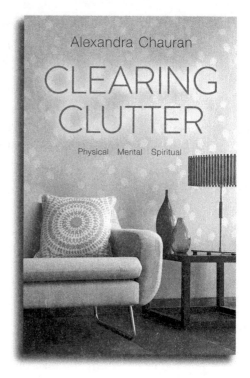

Clearing Clutter
Physical, Mental, and Spiritual
ALEXANDRA CHAURAN

Clutter brings stress to our lives. Whether it's in our home, cubicle, mind, life, or spirit, it's hard to be clearheaded and focused with so much *stuff* stressing us out. *Clearing Clutter* shows you how to clear clutter in all its forms: physical, mental, and spiritual. Feng shui is used when talking about clearing space in your home and creating a good flow of energy. Meditation is used to clear and focus our minds and thoughts and connect to spirit. Organizing and minimizing the physical objects around us brings positivity to each aspect of our lives.

978-0-7387-4227-4, 216 pp., 5 ³⁄₁₆ x 8   **$15.99**

Classical
Feng Shui
for
Health, Beauty
& Longevity

Transform Your Space to Enhance
Well-Being in Body & Home

MASTER DENISE LIOTTA DENNIS

Classical Feng Shui for Health, Beauty & Longevity
Transform Your Space to Enhance Well-Being in Body & Home
MASTER DENISE LIOTTA DENNIS

Improve your wellness, extend your longevity, and secure a healthy environment with the ancient power and wisdom of Classical Feng Shui. This guide provides you with well-researched information about the everyday use of traditional and modern forms of the five elements, empowering you to balance their influence in ways that will make you happier and healthier.

Using the two most popular Classical Feng Shui systems—Flying Stars and Eight Mansions—Master Denise Liotta Dennis presents step-by-step instructions on how to heal and protect both you and your home against detrimental formations. This book features hands-on techniques that you can easily apply to your home and personal situation, helping you achieve a better and more vibrant life.

978-0-7387-4900-6, 312 pp., 6 x 9   **$21.99**

Simple Charms
& Practical Tips for
Creating a Harmonious Home

MAGICAL
HOUSEKEEPING

Tess Whitehurst

Magical Housekeeping
Simple Charms and Practical Tips
for Creating a Harmonious Home
TESS WHITEHURST

Every inch and component of your home is filled with an invisible life force and unique magical energy. *Magical Housekeeping* teaches readers how to sense, change, channel, and direct these energies to create harmony in their homes, joy in their hearts, and success in all areas of their lives.

In this engaging guide, energy consultant and teacher Tess White-hurst shares her secrets for creating an energetically powerful and positive home. Written for those new to metaphysics as well as experienced magical practitioners, *Magical Housekeeping* will teach readers how to summon success, happiness, romance, abundance, and all the desires of the heart. And, by guiding them to make changes in both the seen and unseen worlds simultaneously, this dynamic and delightful book will help activate and enhance readers' intuition and innate magical power.

978-0-7387-1985-6, 240 pp., 5 ³⁄₁₆ x 8   **$16.95**

"Make no mistake, Amy and this book will transform
your life in extraordinary ways."
—Shannon Kaiser, Joy Guru, best-selling author of *Adventures for Your Soul*

Joyful
Living

101 WAYS TO TRANSFORM
YOUR SPIRIT & REVITALIZE
YOUR LIFE

AMY LEIGH MERCREE

Joyful Living
101 Ways to Transform Your Spirit and Revitalize Your Life
AMY LEIGH MERCREE

Experience joy each day and equip yourself for the ups and downs of life with *Joyful Living*, a practical roadmap to achieving inner and outer happiness. Using a mindful and balanced approach, Amy Leigh Mercree presents over a hundred ways to enliven your spirit and step into the blissful life you desire. Featuring affirmations, exercises, inspirational stories, and more, *Joyful Living*'s uplifting entries are easy to use and can be enjoyed in any order. Explore a variety of themes, from spiritual ecstasy to attitudes of gratitude to creative inspiration. Apply mindfulness techniques and work toward greater awareness of the present moment. With this book's guidance, you can calm your busy life and focus on the joyful world around you.

978-0-7387-4659-3, 360 pp., 5 x 7   **$16.99**

LLEWELLYN'S

COMPLETE BOOK OF

MINDFUL LIVING

AWARENESS AND MEDITATION PRACTICES
FOR LIVING IN THE PRESENT MOMENT

Including Michael Bernard Beckwith, Jack Canfield,
Cyndi Dale, Guy Finley, Rolf Gates, and Thomas Moore

ROBERT BUTERA, PhD and ERIN BYRON, MA

Llewellyn's Complete Book of Mindful Living
Awareness & Meditation Practices
for Living in the Present Moment
ROBERT BUTERA, PhD, AND ERIN BYRON, MA

Enhance your awareness, achieve higher focus and happiness, and improve all levels of your health with the supportive practices in this guide to mindful living. Featuring over twenty-five leading meditation and mindfulness experts, *Llewellyn's Complete Book of Mindful Living* shows you how to boost your well-being and overcome obstacles.

With an impressive array of topics by visionary teachers and authors, this comprehensive book provides inspiration, discussion, and specific techniques based on the transformative applications of mindfulness: basic understanding and practices, better health, loving your body, reaching your potential, and connecting to subtle energy and spirit. Using meditation, breathwork, and other powerful exercises, you'll bring the many benefits of mindfulness into your everyday life.

978-0-7387-4677-7, 384 pp., 8 x 10   **$27.99**